Richard Theodore Ely

The social law of service

Richard Theodore Ely

The social law of service

ISBN/EAN: 9783337232887

Printed in Europe, USA, Canada, Australia, Japan

Cover: Foto ©Suzi / pixelio.de

More available books at **www.hansebooks.com**

THE
SOCIAL LAW OF SERVICE

BY

RICHARD T. FLY, Ph.D., LL.D.

PROFESSOR OF POLITICAL ECONOMY AND DIRECTOR OF THE SCHOOL
OF ECONOMICS, POLITICAL SCIENCE, AND HISTORY
IN THE UNIVERSITY OF WISCONSIN

NEW YORK: EATON & MAINS
CINCINNATI: CURTS & JENNINGS
1896

Copyright by
EATON & MAINS,
1896.

Composition, electrotyping,
printing, and binding by
EATON & MAINS,
150 Fifth Ave., New York.

PREFACE.

THIS little volume of essays, the growth of years, deals with topics belonging to that border land in which theology, ethics, and economics meet. Scientifically no territory is more fascinating; practically none can be more important, for it is in this border land that the problems of life present themselves to us.

While the author's aim has been to write a work which the young person of high school attainments may read with profit, possibly even the more mature reader will not in one perusal exhaust all the meaning which has been put into it. May the author, therefore, venture to hope that the present work will find readers who deem it not unworthy of careful study?

The character of the work and the point of view from which it is written have been made so plain in the opening chapter that further words of explanation can scarcely be necessary; and it only remains for the author to express his thanks to those friends who have assisted him with wise criticisms and helpful suggestions.

MADISON, WIS., U. S. A.,
February 19, 1896.

TABLE OF CONTENTS.

CHAPTER I.
OUR FIRM FOUNDATION............................... 11

CHAPTER II.
OUR POINT OF VIEW.................................. 25

CHAPTER III.
THE RELATIONS OF THE OLD AND THE NEW TESTAMENTS SOCIALLY CONSIDERED.................. 49

CHAPTER IV.
THE SOCIAL LAW OF SERVICE......................... 75

CHAPTER V.
THE SOCIAL SIGNIFICANCE OF BAPTISM AND THE LORD'S SUPPER... 103

CHAPTER VI.
SOCIAL SOLIDARITY 125

CHAPTER VII.
OUR NEIGHBORS.................................... 141

CHAPTER VIII.
THE STATE.................................... 157

CHAPTER IX.
MAKING MEN GOOD BY LAW...................... 177

CHAPTER X.
INADEQUACY OF PRIVATE PHILANTHROPY FOR SOCIAL
    REFORM.................................. 191

CHAPTER XI.
OUR EARNINGS................................ 209

CHAPTER XII.
OUR SPENDINGS............................... 223

CHAPTER XIII.
WHAT TO DO.................................. 247

CHAPTER I.
OUR FIRM FOUNDATION.

"How firm a foundation, ye saints of the Lord,
Is laid for your faith in his excellent word!"

THE SOCIAL LAW OF SERVICE.

CHAPTER I.

OUR FIRM FOUNDATION.

ARCHIMEDES was so impressed with the power which even so weak an instrument as man could exert with the aid of the lever that he said, " Give me a place where I may stand, and I will move the earth." What we need, if we would develop principles and rules for the action of ourselves and others in our mutual relations, is solid ground under our feet as a firm foundation. The advantage which those enjoy who have accepted Christ and His Gospel is in this respect immeasurable. Using the figure of the lever, we may say that Christ and His Gospel constitute the lever itself, and that the Church is the fulcrum, and that this lever is sufficient to move the world.

Let us consider more carefully what these statements just made signify. This book is written for those who accept Christ and His

teachings. It is not necessary to argue about
them, because they are taken for granted. In
all systems of conduct, the difficulty is to establish
first principles; when these are granted, the
rest follows easily enough in accordance with
scientific laws. Now, ethical teachers start with
principles of social conduct essentially like those
which we find in the New Testament, but the
difficulty which they all labor under is the establishment
of these first principles. One school of
writers takes as a guiding principle the greatest
amount of happiness. These writers claim that
we should so regulate our conduct that the total
amount of happiness in society may be increased.
If a sacrifice of happiness on my part, which we
may represent as 2a, brings to some one else, or
to others, or to the whole of society—that is, to the
entire world—happiness equal in amount to 3a,
then it is my duty to sacrifice my own happiness
in this case, thereby increasing the total amount
of pleasure or happiness in the world. This is
what is called the utilitarian system of morals.
When it was felt that all sorts of happiness were
not entitled to equal rank, the utilitarian system
was further elaborated by a distinction between
different kinds of happiness, giving us happiness
of a higher and happiness of a lower order. There
can be little doubt that when we build upon these
principles a system of conduct, we shall have

something to guide us in our social relations which accords with the teachings of Christ. But if we ask, "Why?" when each of these fundamental principles is stated, the answer is not altogether easy. Why should I give up my own happiness to increase the total amount of happiness in the world? Why should I divide pleasures into classes and place the pleasures of the mind and spirit above those of the body? What is it which guides me when I distinguish between higher and lower orders of pleasures? Scientific writers upon conduct—that is to say, the ethical philosophers—are divided among themselves when they attempt to give answers to these questions. Their speculations are exceedingly interesting and valuable, and there is no reason why they should be disparaged; but when we want a guide and a support in our life, we feel that we must have a firmer foundation under our feet. The discussions of the scientific writers seem to leave us too much in the air. But when one accepts Christ and His teachings, one can answer the question why we accept our fundamental principles. We say we believe in the law of self-improvement and self-sacrifice because it has been given to us by one whose wisdom and authority we acknowledge.

Christ, Himself, gave us in a few words a fundamental principle which should guide us in our conduct to our fellow-men. The whole duty of man is divided into two parts: the one relating to our duty toward God, and that is that we should love Him with all our heart and mind and soul; and the other is our duty to our fellow-man, and that is that we should love him as we love ourselves. Christ said, "On these two commandments hang all the law and the prophets," meaning that the entire message of God to man was but an elaboration of these principles.

The simplicity of these two fundamental principles has misled many. We may compare them with the axioms and definitions in mathematics. Nothing could be simpler than these axioms and definitions. Everyone will accept it as a mere matter of course that "a whole is greater than any of its parts," and so on with other axioms. Yet, simple as these axioms and definitions are, easily as they are understood even by the schoolboy, they contain in themselves the whole of mathematics; even the higher branches of mathematics, which a very few are capable of grasping, are all involved in the axioms and definitions with which we start. Similarly there may be difficulties, and in modern society there are unquestionably very great difficulties in the elaboration of the "Golden Rule" into a system of conduct which shall solve the problems of life as they thrust themselves upon us. It is not the purpose of the Gospel to render every difficult problem easy. Nothing can be further from the will of Christ than to say, when one faces the problems of modern society, " The Gospel of Christ will solve them," if we then, with this general statement, turn away from an attempt at their solution. It is true that there is no problem of society which the Gospel of Christ will not solve if it is applied. But the question is, What does this Gospel mean now and here in this conflicting chaos of views and obligations? What does it mean for the magistrate and for the legislator? for the railway president? for the president of a college and for a professor? for employers, large and small, and for wage-earners? When any member of a legislative body is asked to fix a rate of wages for public employees somewhat in excess of the competitive rate in order that he may give an upward tendency to wages and help raise the rate generally, is he to do this? Or, is he to take the stand that the taxpayers' interests are paramount? Must he say, " I have no right to use public money to pay more than the lowest competitive rate of wages?" Or shall he say, on the other hand, that organized society has a moral character and is under moral obligations, and that in this matter, as in other matters, he must endeavor to carry out a line of conduct which will promote general well-being? Or, we may take the case of a railway president who has, on the one hand, to consider his stockholders and, on the other, his employees. How do their interests weigh over and against one another? What does the Gospel of Christ teach him in this conflict of interests and apparent conflict of duties? From this Gospel can he elaborate any general principle which will tell him whether wages or dividends should come first in the allotment of the rewards of their joint earnings? Or to what extent, perchance, should the one take the precedence of the other? Take the case of a president of a privately endowed and supported college. Shall he receive every sum of money offered, no matter how this money has been gotten together? If he must ever refuse money, under what circumstances must he refuse it, and under what conditions must he receive it? Shall he say, when certain money is given him, "This represents the gains of iniquity, and I cannot receive it?" Or, shall he make a distinction between those cases in which the iniquity is supported and bolstered up by the acceptance of the gift and the wrongdoer glorified, and those in which the acceptance of the wealth seems to have no bearing upon an encouragement or discouragement of the course of action which resulted in its accumulation? Does it make any difference whether the giver is dead or living, or whether, if living, he comes as a penitent who would make restitution, or one who seeks honor for himself? Again, shall the authorities of an educational institution allow the management of the institution to be influenced consciously by the hope of gifts? Shall certain views be suppressed or only uttered in whispers because they would be likely to give offense to actual or prospective benefactors? Again, is there danger that schools and churches may be even unconsciously perverted by gifts? Do warnings against gifts which are uttered in the Bible ever apply to present conditions? Is there still danger that a gift may " blind the eyes of the wise, and pervert the words of the righteous?"[1] Do we still need to be reminded that with God there is no "taking of gifts?"[2]

Answers to some of these questions may seem easy to the readers of this little work, and answers to others difficult. It is safe to say that they would not be answered by all in precisely the same manner, yet these are by no means the most difficult questions which could be asked. In actual life questions often present themselves in a much more complicated form, and it is precisely characteristic of modern society that the

[1] Deuteronomy xvi, 19 ; also Exodus xxiii, 8.
[2] 2 Chronicles xix, 7.

problems confronting us become more and more complex and difficult. On the other hand, we have in the principles of Christ a secure foundation upon which to build, and we have in the Church sufficient intellect for their solution.

We have, however, something far more than principles. The most powerful social force known to man is religion; beyond anything else, it has shaped and is shaping the world's history. It is the power which leads men to subordinate their own inclinations and interests to the well-being of society. It is something more than this, but it is this among other things. Our religion is not something abstract merely; it is something concrete and living which presents itself in the person of Him who more and more is attaching to Himself the affections of men. It is not any combination of abstract principles, nor is it any number of articles of religion, nine or thirty-nine, that will draw the world, but only a living personality. Christ said, "I, if I be lifted up, will draw all men unto Me." This prediction is in process of realization. Men dispute about creeds, but are more and more filled with admiration for Christ. Workingmen reject with contempt ecclesiasticism, but look to Christ as their leader. And in Christ we have a leader, meek beyond comparison, yet unequaled in strength; gentle, as no one has ever been gentle before, yet unparalleled in sternness; one who presents to us the best qualities of woman, and yet a manliness which is a model to the strongest.

Christ revealed to us the fatherhood of God; and fatherhood means the brotherhood of man. Now, this points us to something else. Brotherhood implies fatherhood, and this also must not be overlooked. Brotherhood cannot be real and genuine without fatherhood.

But our standpoint gives us something further: We must desire social righteousness if we are Christians, and we must work for it. Yet, at times, disappointment is certain to be the outcome of our effort. The way to the attainment of the destiny of society is slow and wearisome, and the struggles which attend our progress are hard. Many begin the journey and turn aside, but the Christian has a twofold source of strength: First, in Christ we have a personal Comforter who affords us consolation in our weariness and disappointments, and we have in Him a Friend whose life was an apparent failure, and apparently as complete a failure when He hung on the cross at Calvary as the world has ever seen. In the second place, we have the assurance that nothing is in reality lost; that we are working for a cause which will finally triumph because, back of it, there stands a Ruler of human destinies. We have thus a sure and steadfast hope.

We know that self-sacrifice is real, and that the individual perishes for the race. This is a literal, scientific truth; yet we have before us the final purpose which is accomplished through the self-sacrifice of countless generations of individuals, and, so far as the individual is concerned, we know that death means life. He that lays down his life, saves it. It is religion which makes possible this sacrifice, and, at the same time, alone makes it rational.

The final triumph of social righteousness is something given to us in countless passages in the Bible, and is something, furthermore, which is implied in our entire standpoint. The Psalmist tells us, "The wicked shall be turned into hell, and all the nations that forget God. For the needy shall not always be forgotten: the expectation of the poor shall not perish forever."[1] And the prophet Isaiah says of Christ, "He shall see of the travail of His soul, and shall be satisfied."[2]

Our standpoint gives us the cross to be borne for our fellows. This may come in many forms; often it comes in part in personal infirmities, weaknesses, and the like; but borne in cheerfulness, it proves a blessing; yet the cross remains.

It may not be too much to say that nothing less than religion can render reforms and reformers safe. It is because religion furnishes a basis

[1] Psalm ix, 17, 18.   [2] Isaiah liii, 11.

and an enduring hope, and at the same time furnishes restraints. It points out the only sure road to success in social reform. Those who have not this help and this hope are liable to mistakes which have been witnessed in thousands and thousands of cases; frequently they grow weary in well-doing because the coming of the Kingdom is delayed, and turn aside from their high purpose. On the other hand, some seeing the slowness with which the methods of peace accomplish their purpose, feel inclined to resort to methods of force, and the propaganda of anarchy is the result.

CHAPTER II.
OUR POINT OF VIEW.

"MANY nations have believed in gods of mixed or positively malignant character. Other nations have, indeed, ascribed to their deities all the admirable qualities they could conceive, but benevolence was not one of these. They have believed in gods that were beautiful, powerful, immortal, happy, but not benevolent."—*Sir J. R. Seeley, Natural Religion, p.* 13.

"But the Ethics of the Greeks were at the best narrow and egoistical. Morality, however exalted or comprehensive, only seemed to embrace the *individual;* it was extremely incomplete as regards the family; and had scarcely any suspicion of what we call social relations. No Greek ever attained the sublimity of such a point of view. The highest point he could attain was to conduct *himself* according to just principles; he never troubled himself with others. By the introduction of Christianity, Ethics became Social as well as Individual."—*George Henry Lewes, Biographical History of Philosophy, Vol. I, Conclusion of Ancient Philosophy, pp.* 337, 338.

CHAPTER II.

OUR POINT OF VIEW.

EVERY great advance in science has had as its beginning and first cause a new point of view. Every epoch-making discovery has implied a way of looking at things different from that which has previously prevailed. As the world's civilization advances new points of view prevail. Great stages in the evolution of religion are characterized by progressively better points of view. The great lights in the world's history give us new points of view. Every system of philosophy or religion has its point of view which is a key to its comprehension.

The Copernican system of astronomy reversed the old way of looking at the earth, the sun, and the planets. Copernicus asserted that the sun was the center about which the earth and the planets revolved. The correctness of this system was thoroughly established by Kepler, Galileo, and, above all, Newton. It was a glorious achievement, and it lies at the basis of subsequent progress in this branch of knowledge. William Harvey, in the seventeenth century, dis-

covered the circulation of the blood, and this
gave a point of view which was epoch-making in
the knowledge of the human body. Lavoisier
overthrew the theory of combustion based upon
an escape of a substance called phlogiston, and
showed that combustion was an act of combination with oxygen. He demonstrated that in
combustion the weight of the product was equal
to the sum of the weight of the substance burned
and the oxygen used up. His great instrument
was the balance which had previously been neglected, and he thus introduced the quantitative
period of chemistry. This was a new point of
view which gave an immense impetus to chem-
ical knowledge. Charles Darwin's vast contribution to knowledge consists in the doctrine of
evolution which has been and is being applied
to every branch of knowledge, even to religion,
with astonishing results. Error has been mixed
with truth in the immense intellectual activity to
which Darwin's point of view has given rise, but
it will in the end be seen that probably the work
of few men who have ever lived has so advanced
the intellectual progress, and perhaps, also, the
social progress, of the race. Yet it was all given
in the point of view.

If we would understand the Christian religion
we must have the point of view of Christ. What
was it which distinguished His message to the

race from that of all other religious teachers, and made it infinitely more fruitful of good? There is one word which will sum it all up, and that is, love—love of a different sort from anything which the world had known. The revelation of Christ was the revelation of love. It manifested itself, however, in two different aspects: a Godward and a manward aspect.

Now, it is our purpose to consider rather the second manifestation of love, but we cannot neglect entirely the first. It has been well pointed out that the God revealed to us by Christ is something quite different from the gods worshiped by Greece and Rome and all the nations of antiquity, save the Jews. The gods of Greece and Rome did not give men their highest ideas and ideals of character and right conduct. The priests of ancient religions were not the leaders of nations in what was highest and best, but there were philosophers with higher ideas and ideals than those given them by their gods.[1]

There was revealed to the Jews a God who could command the devotion of the heart and soul and mind of men, the contemplation of whose attributes could not fail to elevate all His worshipers. This was a God who loved all men,

[1] This is well brought out in *Religion in History and in Modern Life*, by Rev. A. M. Fairbairn, D.D., Principal of Mansfield College, Oxford.

and therefore hated human sacrifice and the abomination of the heathen nations which always meant cruelty to men; a God whose purpose it was, through Israel, to bless all the nations of the world. Now, this true God was revealed more fully to men through Christ. There is no break between the revelation of Christ and that of the Old Testament in this respect, but the Gospel of Christ was a further unfolding of the earlier revelation. Christ revealed to us the fatherhood of God, and Max Müller regards this as the distinctive peculiarity of Christianity.

While His doctrine of the ruler of the universe was the basis of Christ's entire message, yet His point of view is given pre-eminently in His new view of man. It is, in fact, this new view of man which reflects back light upon His revelation of the character of God. How, indeed, otherwise can we understand the opening words of the Lord's Prayer, "Our Father?"

Christ taught the infinite worth of every human individual, and our endless mutual obligations, so that after we have done our utmost for our fellow-men we must still say that we are unprofitable servants. The distinctive feature of Christ's teaching from the human standpoint is the exaltation of man, carrying with it universal benevolence as a supreme law of conduct. Christ thus furnishes a strange contrast to all who ever went before Him, and became literally the first philanthropist, as He has well been called by a distinguished historian.¹ These words sound strange to modern ears at the present time when we have become so accustomed to philanthropy, both genuine and spurious. We find, indeed, much philanthropy outside the visible Church, and there are those who deny the claims of Christ, and yet exercise philanthropy, unconscious that their ruling motive has been derived from the Leader whom they misunderstand and deny. When we read in the biography of a man in a religious paper that, *although* he was a philanthropist, he was at the same time a professed Christian and church member, we may think that the separation between organized Christianity and philanthropy has gone far. But without philanthropy there never would have been a Christian Church, and without Christ we would have had no philanthropy.

It is hard to grasp the fact that we are here dealing with literal, historical truth; but the author has to say that the more he thought about this subject, the more he has read about it, the more he has looked into the opinions of various authorities who have given attention to it, the more strongly he is impressed with the fact that Christ was the first philanthropist. We

¹ The author of *Ecce Homo*.

hear about the Stoics and about Gotama Buddha, and we are told that in them we find a philanthropy like that of Christ; but it is only necessary to look more carefully into their teachings to ascertain that we have to do with something very different, as we shall see presently. The author of *Ecce Homo* says: "Though there was humanity among the ancients, there was no philanthropy. In other words, humanity was known to them as an occasional impulse and not as a standing rule of life. A case of distress made painfully manifest and prominent would often excite compassion; the feeling might lead to a single act of benevolence; but it had not strength enough to give birth to reflection, or to develop itself into a compassion for other persons equally distressed, whose distresses were not equally manifest. Exceptional sufferings had, therefore, a chance of relief; but the ordinary sufferings, which affected whole classes of men, excited no pity, and were treated as a part of the natural order of things, providential dispensations which it might even be impious to endeavor to counteract." If space were sufficient, many illustrations could be given to show the radical difference between Christianity on its manward side and the teachings of other religions and of ancient philosophers; but, as it is, only two or three striking contrasts can be adduced. Let us take Brahmanism, which has governed for centuries the life of millions of human beings: In contrast to the brotherhood of men and their essential equality in the sight of God, the Father of them all, we have the doctrine that one class of men comes from the mouth of God and are forever superior to all other classes of men from whom they are separated by a line which it is the height of impiety to cross. The Brahmans are raised so high above other men that a man who strikes one of them but with a blade of grass is regarded as worthy the condemnation of hell. Now, below the Brahmans there is another class, or caste, created from the arms of God; below these there is still another class of men created from the thighs of God, and below these there is still a class, the Sudras, springing from the feet of God, and these are regarded as unworthy even to read the Brahman scriptures. But even now we are not at the end, because below this lowest class we have those who belong to no class—the Pariahs, veritable outcasts. Thus we have the Indian system of castes, which is an essential part of the Indian religion.

The nations which previous to Christ attained the highest degree of civilization were the Greeks and the Romans, and it would probably be admitted that among them three of the most enlightened and, at the same time, humane men were—of the Greeks, Plato and Aristotle, and of the Romans, the orator and philosopher, Cicero. Plato is so far from regarding all men as embraced in one universal brotherhood, that he divides them into classes, separate and distinct in very nature. We find in Plato, men of gold, men of silver, men of brass, and men of clay; and the lower orders subsist for the gain of the higher orders. The English authority on Plato, Professor Jowett, states that in Plato we find few traces of even humanity to slaves,[1] and humanity, as we have seen, occupies a far lower rank than philanthropy. Slavery was accepted and defended as a permanent basis of civilization, and so far was Plato from the universality of Christ, that he looked upon all the human race, outside the Greeks, as naturally slaves.

Aristotle was in theory and practice a man who must rank high among the ancients on account of his humanity, yet, in speaking of men in general, he says: "The lower sort are by nature slaves, and it is better for them, as for all inferiors, that they should be under the rule of a master. . . . The use made of slaves, or of tame animals, is not very different; for both

---

[1] See Jowett's Translation of Plato, vol. 5, p. xciv.
Jowett himself says that Christ first " taught men to love their enemies."—*College Sermons*, p. 165.

with their bodies minister to the needs of life. It is clear, then, that some men are by nature free, and others slaves, and that for these latter, slavery is both expedient and right." [1]

Cicero, the ethical philosopher, asks the question, Who would not slay ten slaves of whom one had been guilty of murder, rather than let the guilty one escape? It seems to him far better that nine innocent slaves should suffer death than that the guilty one should escape.

Need we bring all this in contrast with the whole life and teachings of Christ? Surely all the words of Christ, and the whole life of Christ from beginning to end, bring us into a different world of thought and feeling. Christ taught us universal, all-embracing love, and so far was He from regarding the lower orders as created simply to subserve the gain of the higher orders, that He especially enjoined upon the higher to use their superiority to elevate the lower orders, even those most wretched and degraded. He, Himself, set the example in the lowly office of washing the feet of His disciples, and told them that "Whosoever will be great among you, let him be your minister; and whosoever will be chief among you, let him be your servant: even as the Son of man came not to be ministered unto, but to minister, and to give His

[1] Aristotle's *Politics*, translated by Jowett, I, c. 5, §§ 8–11.

life a ransom for many." [1] Christ habitually associates with the poor and the outcasts, and this is something so strange and unusual that His contemporaries cannot grasp the principle upon which He acted, for they express their constant astonishment and also their condemnation. It was a strange leader among the Jews who loved to associate with publicans and sinners. But notice this: When John the Baptist asked for proofs of the Messiahship of Christ, those which Jesus offered were His ministry unto weak and feeble folk. We all remember how John, when in prison, sent two of his disciples to Christ, "And said unto Him, Art thou He that should come, or do we look for another?" And how Jesus answered, "Go and show John again those things which ye do hear and see: the blind receive their sight, and the lame walk, the lepers are cleansed, and the deaf hear, the dead are raised up, and the poor have the Gospel preached to them." [2]

But note this, further: Christ describes the last judgment when He gathers about Him all the nations of the earth, separating them one from another like a shepherd dividing his sheep from his goats. But what is the test? Ministry to the lowly, to the abandoned, to the outcast; feeding the hungry, giving drink to the thirsty, clothing the naked, visiting those sick and those

---

[1] Matthew xx, 26–28.   [2] Matthew xi, 2–5.

in prison. Brahmanism says: "He who strikes a Brahman with a blade of grass is worthy of hell." Christ says those who neglect to minister unto the lowest of the needy and wretched of earth shall be cast away into everlasting punishment.

But we must consider at somewhat greater length Buddhism and Stoicism, because these two are held to have the strongest claim to rank with Christianity with respect to altruism.

Buddhism has received much praise lately, and has even found adherents in Christian lands. It is claimed that Buddhism inculcates a lofty philanthropy like that of Christianity, and choice selections from the sacred writings of Buddhism give a show of color for this assertion. We read, for example, that toward the close of his life, Siddârtha or Gotama Buddha, the founder of Buddhism, addressed his followers in these words: "Beloved mendicants, if you revere my memory, love all the disciples as you love me and my doctrines." Another saying of Gotama Buddha is this: "As even at the risk of her own life a mother watches over her child, her only child, let him [that is, the Buddhist saint] exercise good will without measure toward all beings." Still another saying reminds us of the eulogy of love written by the Apostle Paul in the thirteenth chapter of First Corinthians: "If a man live a hundred years and spend the whole of his time in religious attentions and offerings, . . . all this is not equal to an act of pure love."

Now we will not criticise the favorable presentations of Buddhism which have recently been made, nor will we attempt at present to show how probable it is that the glory of Christianity has been reflected back on Buddhism, making it brilliant with a brilliancy not its own. Let us take Buddhism at its best and gratefully acknowledge all its services, its sympathy with all created things, and its devotion to the good of men and animals, and ask ourselves the question: Have we in Buddhism a real and genuine philanthropy like that revealed in Christ?

First: The end of Buddhism is escape from the pains of existence in Nirvâna, which, if it be existence at all and not annihilation—a disputed point—is an existence as impersonal as that of the jellyfish floating on a quiet sea of peace, and "drinking in the warm fluid in a state of lazy, blissful repose."[1] The end of Christianity is life, more life, and yet ever more life, spent in service.

Second: The altruism of Buddhism is largely based on a desire for the suppression of the ego—of self. Self-assertion means desire, and desire brings continued existence from which Buddhism seeks relief. The suppression of self, and thus

[1] Sir Monier Williams's *Buddhism*, p. 141.

the cessation of the possibility of service to others, is its ideal. Christianity means the suppression of selfishness, but the enlargement of self in service.

Third: Buddhism knows no personal fatherhood of God. The God of Gotama Buddha was "the Unknowable," for only the laws of nature could be known in obedience to which Nirvâna might be found. Christianity gives us the fatherhood of God, a condition of genuine brotherhood, and brotherhood is the basis of altruism. Buddhism takes away the very foundation of philanthropy.

Fourth: Buddhism is essentially a philosophy of individualism, whereas social solidarity is an essential part of Christianity. In Buddhism each man stands alone. Karma, justice, rules all; everything which we suffer comes to us from a guilty past in our present existence, or some one of innumerable past existences. From Karma no one can release us. We work out our own salvation in self-culture, self-abnegation, self-crucifixion, and cessation of rebirths when Nirvâna is reached. Christianity binds men together in sin and in salvation. Heredity and environment encircle us all with common ties. Christianity in its very essence is a social religion. Buddhism is self-centered; Christianity directs attention outward to others. The salvation of Buddhism is a purely individual salvation; the salvation of Christ is a social salvation as well as an individual salvation.

Fifth: Buddhism seeks escape from this world and directs conduct to this end. Its rules of action are preparation for future nonexistence, or at best semipersonal existence. At any rate, Buddhism directs attention away from this world; its religion is "otherworldliness." Christianity teaches eternal life, but eternal life begun now in the present world and gained in a right use of the present world. "If you would live with Christ in the next world, you must live like Christ in this world."[1] This otherworldliness of Buddhism weakens essentially its philanthropy.

We cannot dwell long on Stoicism, which, like Buddhism, we are considering only in one of its aspects. There is much that is grand and noble in it, and for this we are grateful. There is no reason why we should hesitate to give it its full share of praise. Christianity is not contrary to the best in other religious beliefs and in other philosophical systems, but it is simply superior to all others. It is an unfolding as well as a revelation. What is highest and purest outside of Christianity but strengthens Christianity. The three Stoics most quoted are Seneca, a contemporary of the Apostle Paul, and Epictetus and

[1] Charles Kingsley.

Marcus Aurelius, of the second century of our era. It seems to the present writer not improbable that sayings of Christ and His apostles and something of the spirit of Christianity may have reached these Stoics. He is aware of the grounds urged against this view, but does not regard them as sufficient. However, this is a minor matter.

First of all, Stoicism was a philosophy for a select few and Christianity a life for all. The fact that no effort was made to extend to all men the benefits of the Stoic philosophy shows that the loftiest of the Stoics were not animated by the philanthropy of Christ. Second: The fatherhood of God was not an essential part of the Stoic philosophy. God was nature, a great Power to be obeyed, obeyed cheerfully, but a Power not to be moved by human wants, desires, and petitions. If an idea of a closer relation than a cold one to nature is discovered among the Stoics, this idea is neither habitual nor vital. Third: The brotherhood of man as taught is weak. We are children of Zeus, the father of us all, it is said; but does this mean more than that we are all products of great natural forces? We are all partakers in common reason. We should regard all men as fellow-citizens of our world and abstain from unkindness. The benevolence toward all men of the Stoics was chiefly negative. A doctrine like the Christian doctrine of sins of omission in our relations to our fellows is something which cannot be found in Stoicism. "Inasmuch as ye did it not," Christ said, but philanthropy of this kind was something that not even Marcus Aurelius taught. Fourth: Stoicism was cold, impassive, self-centered. Its ideal was in some respects like that of Buddhism. Self-centered superiority to the passions of life, passive acceptance of the allotments of a Superior Power, an unruffled temper in time of prosperity and time of adversity—these were ideals, and their attainment was an individual work. The Stoic was, too, an individualist. Yet not always did the Stoic counsel passive acceptance, because when life offered nothing and duties to friends did not hold one back, suicide was a wise act. As has been well said, Stoicism, like the philosophy of many Oriental nations, was barely above the suicide mark. Shall we then be led away by comparisons of this cold philosophy with the life-giving power of Christianity, Christianity which means fullness of life for self and for others?

A college-bred woman, a friend of the author, gives in the following words her own experience in an attempt to find a refuge in Stoicism:

"Originally I had derived a great deal of happiness from the commonplaces of everyday life, but the continued ill health of those with whom I was associated baffled all plans for the future and present.

"The problem was how to live and meet successfully the disappointments that the future was certain to bring, with no possible hope of physical recovery for the one dearest to me and all that that entailed.

"The only sane conduct for me seemed to be to keep myself steeled against delusive hopes and nerved up to meet every possible disappointment.

"For two years I tried most conscientiously to be a Stoic, holding myself self-poised to meet every emergency. There is no doubt that I gained greatly in self-control; but the range of my life became so restricted as to become finally unbearable.

"This was the result that might have been foreseen, but I failed to see it.

"If it was the greatest virtue to be self-contained and self-controlled, then it was as great a virtue for others to be self-contained; reliance on self was as salutary for others as for me, and the altruistic attempt to benefit others might not help—indeed, it might hinder—their progress toward self-dependence. There was not the demand or occasion for personal contact and helpfulness that there was before. My interests became more circumscribed and self-centered; the intense individualism of the Stoic ideal steadily undermined my interests in others, until my life became so intolerably narrow to me that in self-defense I was compelled to discard altogether the Stoic ideal of life.

"I had learned self-dependence, but with it my life had become pauperized."

Anything so fundamental as our religious convictions must find expression in all our activities, and the absence of the Christ-view, exalting man, is discerned in the art, literature, and customs of all heathen lands. Bishop Westcott, with his deep insight, observes that in the " marvelous products of Indian industries at Kensington . . . you will search in vain, I think, in all that multitudinous display of ornament, rich in exquisite harmonies of colors and in delicacy of patient skill, for one trace of reverence for man. Every human form . . . there . . . is either grotesque or hideous." [1]

If, with this point of view in mind, which our comparisons have brought out, we read the entire New Testament, we shall see many things which have escaped our attention heretofore. We shall find that God's commands to man are not arbitrary, but that they have their ground in the welfare of man. This is plainly stated over and

[1] Bishop B. F. Westcott, *Social Aspects of Christianity*, p 59.

over again. There is an inclination on the part of many to make a distinction between things wrong in themselves, and things which somehow are wrong, but are not wrong in themselves. Among those wrongs of a lesser order it will be found that men place those acts which bear hardly on others; those things which grieve and injure others. But we are taught plainly by Christianity that the purpose of the most fundamental laws is the welfare of men, and in the promotion of this welfare we find the unity of all those laws which regulate our social conduct.

Why should we not steal? The answer will probably be because God has commanded us to abstain from theft; but St. Paul does not hesitate to give us a human reason: "Let him that stole," says the apostle, "steal no more; but rather let him labor, working with his hands the thing which is good, that he may have to give to him that needeth."[1] What does this mean? It signifies that the thief engages in conduct which is socially negative; he destroys wealth; instead of contributing to others, he takes from others. He is enjoined to cease this negative line of conduct, and to engage in positive, constructive work. And for what purpose? In order that as a result of his work he may have to give to him that needeth.

[1] Ephesians iv, 28.

Why should we speak the truth? St. Paul says, because "we are members one of another."[1] As it is put by another,[2] "untruthfulness is an offense against our fellowship in Christ."

But how this point of view throws light on many other injunctions which have proved a stumbling-block! Why should women adorn themselves in "modest apparel," with "shamefacedness and sobriety;" not with "braided hair, or gold, or pearls, or costly array?" When an answer is given which implies asceticism, it provokes a rebellious feeling. Why should not we enjoy all these good things of the world? When this sort of an answer is given it is seen to be in clear contradiction of the general tenor of Christ's teachings. But the apostle did not stop at this point; he added an explanation for his command, telling us plainly that it was becoming in women, professing godliness, to adorn themselves with good works.[3] The other kind of adornment did two things contrary to the law of love: First, it turned attention away from one's fellows, from social duties—and can we not see this to-day all about us?—and, furthermore, it consumed that substance which could be used to minister to the needy.

Our point of view gives us a guide for individ-

---

[1] Ephesians iv, 25.   [2] Bishop B. F. Westcott.
[3] 1 Timothy ii, 8–10.

Our Point of View. 47

ual reform and social reconstruction. It puts new meaning into what St. Paul tells: "And if I bestow all my goods to feed the poor, and if I give my body to be burned, but have not love, it profiteth me nothing."[1] In fact, it profiteth nobody anything. It does no good to the world. Giving without love has so degenerated that the very word " charity " has become an offense, and men ask if benevolence has not done more harm than good. Giving may have done more harm than good; not benevolence. Love makes fruitful giving possible. That is, perhaps, the one great lesson of Tolstoi's *What to Do*. But love bridges over the chasm between human souls, and makes it—if more blessed to give than to receive—still a blessing to receive, for under the law of love, both giving and receiving are directed by a wisdom born of loving thought and care. This is the lesson which we must learn over and over again, coming back continually to the point of view of Christ.

[1] 1 Corinthians, xiii, 3.

CHAPTER III.

THE RELATIONS OF THE OLD AND THE NEW TESTAMENTS SOCIALLY CONSIDERED.

"MORE than once did the Hebrew kings seek to break away from the intermeddling of the clergy; but God smote the politician and not the prophet. . . . Saul meddled with Samuel's duties, and God took his kingdom from him. But Samuel was never censured for his intermeddling with the affairs of Saul. David had to submit to the authority of more than one priest. No priest was ever compelled to silence before him. Isaiah, Ezekiel, Jeremiah, Hosea, Amos, all the preachers of righteousness dwelt on social and civil sins. They dwelt on hardly anything else."—*Bishop G. Haven, National Sermons.*

"The great idea that the Bible is the history of mankind's deliverance from all tyranny, outward as well as inward; of the Jews, as the one free constitutional people among a world of slaves and tyrants; of their ruin, as the righteous fruit of a voluntary return to despotism; of the New Testament, as the good news that freedom, brotherhood, and equality, once confided only to Judæa and to Greece, and dimly seen even there, was henceforth to be the right of all mankind, the law of all society—who was there to tell me that? Who is there now to go forth and tell it to the millions who have suffered and doubted and despaired like me, and turn the hearts of the disobedient to the wisdom of the just, before the great and terrible day of the Lord come? Again I ask—who will go forth and preach that Gospel, and save his native land?" —*Charles Kingsley, Alton Locke, p.* 323.

CHAPTER III.

THE RELATIONS OF THE OLD AND THE NEW TESTAMENTS SOCIALLY CONSIDERED.

ONE of the marked features of Biblical study at the present time is the increased attention given to the Old Testament. This is most fortunate, for the New Testament cannot be understood except as a growth out of the Old. The social teachings, however, of the New Testament have not as yet by anyone been brought into sufficiently close connection with the social law of the Hebrews, and consequently those teachings are only inadequately grasped, even when not fully misinterpreted. The cry has been raised, " Back to Christ," but to go back to the real teachings of Christ we must go back to the Old Testament.[1]

It cannot be our purpose in this little book to treat this subject exhaustively, for that would require vast study and a large work. Certain suggestions, however, may be thrown out which

[1] Some say the rallying cry should be, "Forward to Christ." This is equally true, but it is, after all, expressing the same idea, only in other words.

will prove helpful as a guide to thought and study.

The purpose of all the laws and regulations of both the Old and the New Testaments is undoubtedly the glory of God and the welfare of man in society; or, more simply, the welfare of society. But the Bible teaches us more and more clearly, as we proceed in Biblical history, that the glory of God means the welfare of society. We can do nothing for God, Himself, whose are all the riches of the earth; "the cattle on a thousand hills," as the Psalmist sings; but we can do something for his creatures, and all divine institutions have a social purpose.

If we take up the Old Testament and read it, we find that we have in it the history of Israel. In this history we have laws and regulations for the upbuilding of a national morality, but with glimpses of something larger. The promise was to Abraham that in him all the nations of the earth should be blessed;[1] and this larger view was something which was never entirely lost from the consciousness of the wisest and best in the nation.

The religion of the Jews was designed for the welfare of society, furnishing a sanction for social conduct in the individual. Of this the greatest and best in Israel had a keen consciousness.

[1] Genesis xvii, 18.

The Old and New Testaments. 53

The nation and the glories of the nation filled the minds and hearts of those Israelites in whom God was represented as specially well pleased. And reference is always had to provision made for the weak and the feeble. This is the peculiar glory of Israel, making Israel stand out in bold relief from the other nations of antiquity. This is the meaning of the land laws, of the usury laws, of the regulations of the year of Jubilee and other laws of this kind: "And when ye reap the harvest of your land, thou shalt not make clean riddance of the corners of thy field when thou reapest, neither shalt thou gather any gleaning of thy harvest: thou shalt leave them unto the poor, and to the stranger."[1] David said: "I have been young, and now am old; yet have I not seen the righteous forsaken, nor his seed begging bread." This was a natural outcome of the law of Israel, and must always be the case when righteous social laws prevail. It was all this which made the law of Israel a delight in which one could "meditate day and night;" a fortress, a bulwark, a protection against every vicissitude of fortune. Think what this means! Does anyone ever sing the praises in these tones of a modern code?

And when the law ceased to carry out the divine purposes, God's wrath is kindled and His

[1] Leviticus xxiii, 22.

prophets proclaim His anger in thunder tones: "Rise up, ye women that are at ease. . . . Many days and years shall ye be troubled, ye careless women: . . . Upon the land of my people shall come up thorns and briers. . . . The palaces shall be forsaken; the multitude of the city shall be left; the forts and towers shall be for dens forever, a joy of wild asses, a pasture of flocks; until the Spirit be poured upon us from on high, and the wilderness be a fruitful field, and the fruitful field be counted for a forest.

"Then judgment shall dwell in the wilderness, and righteousness remain in the fruitful field. And the work of righteousness shall be peace; and the effect of righteousness, quietness and assurance forever."[1]

Still clearer are verses from another chapter, namely, chapter v: "And now go to; I will tell you what I will do to my vineyard: I will take away the hedge thereof, and it shall be eaten up; and break down the wall thereof, and it shall be trodden down:

"And I will lay it waste: it shall not be pruned, nor digged; but there shall come up briers and thorns: I will also command the clouds that they rain no rain upon it.

"For the vineyard of the Lord of hosts is the

[1] Isaiah xxxii, 9–17.

house of Israel, and the men of Judah his pleasant plant: and he looked for judgment, but behold oppression; for righteousness, but behold a cry.

"Woe unto them that join house to house, that lay field to field, till there be no place, that they may be placed alone in the midst of the earth!

"In mine ears said the Lord of hosts, Of a truth many houses shall be desolate, even great and fair, without inhabitant."[1]

Turning to Jeremiah, chapter v, we have the heading, "Judgments upon the Jews."[2] The chapter opens with these words: "Run ye to and fro through the streets of Jerusalem, and see now, and know, and seek in the broad places thereof, if ye can find a man, if there be any that executeth judgment, that seeketh the truth; and I will pardon it."

Then we have specifications, as idolatry and adultery, then denunciations and warnings; then in verses 25-29 we find these words:

"Your iniquities have turned away these things, and your sins have withholden good things from you.

"For among my people are found wicked men: they lay wait, as he that setteth snares; they set a trap, they catch men.

[1] Isaiah v, 5-9.   [2] Chapter v, 1, and 25-29.

"As a cage is full of birds, so are their houses full of deceit: therefore they are become great, and waxen rich.

"They are waxen fat, they shine: yea, they overpass the deeds of the wicked: they judge not the cause, the cause of the fatherless, yet they prosper; and the right of the needy do they not judge.

"Shall I not visit for these things? saith the Lord: shall not my soul be avenged on such a nation as this?"

We cannot understand the separation of the Jews from other nations, and the strong condemnation of the practices of these other nations, unless we know at the same time what those practices carried with them. We do not for a moment deny that God wished for Himself the services of Israel. It is repeatedly declared that God is a jealous God. But warnings against idolatry have also a social significance which is brought out clearly when it is ascertained what the worship of false gods carried with it. The abominations of all sorts which are condemned, embraced immorality of every kind, often a very part of the worship of the false gods; cruelties of every description, including even human sacrifice.

The office of the Jews was to establish right relations among themselves, first for themselves,

The Old and New Testaments. 57

then for others. The nation is God's instrument for the establishment of universal righteousness. "In many epochs of the world, nationalism is often the truest universalism."[1] This is not the place to enter into an exhaustive discussion of the treatment which the heathen nations received at the hands of the Jews, yet a few thoughts in the present connection may prove helpful. The Jewish nation conceived it to be its mission to punish and exterminate utterly certain corrupt and depraved tribes. First, let us remember that in all ages the nation has control over life and death, and that that is righteous in the nation which is criminal in the individual. This holds with respect to property as well as person. This is recognized by religious teachers of all ages, as well as the greatest political philosophers who have ever lived. The nation is an instrument in carrying out God's plans, and it need not excite astonishment if the mission is given to the Jews to exterminate utterly debased and depraved nations, whose degradation has proceeded so far that their condition is a hopeless one. It it said, to be sure, that the innocent suffer with the guilty. That must always be so in this world.

---

[1] Rev. W. H. Fremantle, D.D., *The World as the Subject of Redemption*, second edition, p. 76. It can scarcely be necessary to remark that universalism here means much the same thing as cosmopolitanism.

It is a part of the social solidarity which is one of the profoundest laws of the world, and brings before us a truth of science, of history, and of religion, namely, that there is no such thing as a purely individual sin.[1]

The difficulties which so many persons have with the Old Testament, in so far as these difficulties pertain to the relations between the Jews and other nations, are largely due to a one-sided religion. We have of late been led by an extreme reaction against neglect of the individual in Church and State to lose any keen consciousness of what Church and State mean. We have to do in the Old Testament with God's dealings with nations rather than individuals who were reached through the nation. But if our teachers no longer know what the nation means, if they have no idea of the part which in past history the nation has played in the work of God in the world, if they do not perceive that God is still working through the nation in the redemption of the world, if they have no sense of the gradual unfolding of God's purpose and of the growth of righteousness in the world such as is indicated by Christ's words, "first the blade, then the ear, after that the full corn in the ear;"

---

[1] Those who are interested in the study of this point are referred to two great works by Professor von Oettingen, *Die Moralstatistik*, and *Die Christliche Sittenlehre*.

The Old and New Testaments. 59

then how can we wonder if in their flocks there are many who are distressed and troubled by that which cannot be understood by those who look upon each individual as a disconnected atom and not as one of a family, a member of a nation, and a part of humanity?

One or two further suggestions may be offered. There have been wars in the past in all lands, and wars still continue. Much as these are to be deplored, earnestly as we may strive for the abolition of war, we must acknowledge that through war as well as peace human progress has been achieved. Every historian asserts this. Can we then fail to say that in our world, composed of weak, ignorant, sinful men, wars have been a part of God's plans for mankind? If we have any knowledge of the general conditions of the world at the time when the Jewish nation made war upon foreign tribes and nations, we know that they were not ripe for the message of international peace. Moreover, we are plainly taught that God's messages were adapted to their condition. As Christ said, Moses suffered certain things because of the hardness of their hearts. Consequently war and conquest were not forbidden, but an effort was made to render war far more humane than it was among the oriental nations, and what was commanded the Jews in this respect was a marvelous advance on what had been and still was customary. Limits were set to cupidity as a motive of conquest in the command not to take the silver and gold on the graven images,[1] and a more considerate treatment of foreigners living among them in a state of bondage was urged, than was taught by the most enlightened of the Greeks and Romans before the time of Christ.

Even while we second with all our might efforts to establish peace among nations, it would be rash in the extreme to say that war has now accomplished its purpose while oriental barbarities such as have recently been witnessed in Armenia still continue. And what, indeed, has maintained the power of Turkey in this century? Is it the gentleness and love of the Christian nations of Europe? Quite to the contrary. The fear of rival nations in commercial competition; in other words, the lust of gold has been a potent factor in bolstering up the iniquity of the Turk. And will Christians lament the fact if in the fullness of time, in bloody war, the power of Turkey is annihilated and ceases to curse the earth? Yet Turkey is far more enlightened, far more humane in her ordinary transactions, in her usual civic life, than the depraved nations who,

---

[1] Deuteronomy vii, 25. Compare the sermon, "The Nation and the Church," by Frederick Denison Maurice, in *The Patriarchs and Lawgivers of the Old Testament.*

after they had made full the cup of their iniquities, were destroyed by the Jews.

The sacrifices and entire worship of the Jews were national as well as individual. No one could set up a church or a religious establishment for himself. The ordinance of circumcision, which was compulsory, was designed, among other things, at any rate, to indicate national solidarity in all its phases, religious and ethical.

The New Testament is a continuation of the old dispensation, but with certain marked differences. The social law of the Old Testament, which was designed to establish right relations among the Hebrews, we distinguish from the ceremonial law. The New Testament did two things with respect to that social law of the Old Testament which was designed to establish right relations among men. First of all, it universalized this social law; a national morality was no longer sufficient; the idea of ethical obligation, it has been said, is conterminous with the idea of society. Heretofore society was exclusively national, and morality was essentially national. Christianity replaces the national society with a world-wide society and makes morality universal. Our duty is no longer to those of our own house, or even of our own nation, but it is to all the world.

Christian thought has so permeated our life

that it is hard for us to understand how difficult it was for a Jew to comprehend this idea of a universal society; yet, in passing, we may observe that it was easier for a Jew than it would have been for a Greek.

It was necessary for Christ and His apostles to come back, again and again, to this idea of universal society and the corresponding extension of ethical obligation, and approach the same subject from every standpoint; and even then the idea was only slowly grasped. It was one which had gradual growth among the immediate disciples of Christ; one which was resisted strenuously by the new adherents of these disciples among the Jews, and one which awakened intensest anger on the part of the Jews in general.

Christ illustrates the universality of human relations and brotherhood in the parable of the Good Samaritan. "Who is my neighbor?" The answer is given, Everyone who needs my help. Moreover, it is a condition of salvation that I should render help to the needy one. Before His crucifixion, Christ said, "I will draw all men unto Me." After His resurrection He gave commandment to His disciples, "Go ye, therefore, and teach all nations."

The teachings and deeds of the twelve apostles, as recorded in the New Testament, show how gradually this truth was received. It re-

The Old and New Testaments. 63

quired a vision to persuade Peter to enter the house of Cornelius, "one of another nation." At last, the universal nature of Christ's religion seemed to dawn upon Peter, and he said, "Of a truth I perceive that God is no respecter of persons: but in every nation he that feareth Him, and worketh righteousness, is accepted with Him."[1]

The Jews were astonished when they found that on the Gentiles was poured out the gift of the Holy Ghost. The Apostle Paul was able to obtain a hearing when, from the stairs of the castle, he made his great speech to the Jews in Jerusalem, until he announced the message which had come unto him to go unto the Gentiles, and then they "lifted up their voices, and said, Away with such a fellow from the earth: for it is not fit that he should live."[2]

Now, the second thing which Christ did for the social law establishing right relations among men, was to intensify and elevate it. If we speak of the Christian revelation in the first respect as the "extension" of the social law, we may speak of it in the second respect as its "intension." This intension of the law is clear throughout the utterances of Christ. Christ opposes what He said to what Moses and their traditions had told the Jews. Again and again he uses the words:

[1] Acts x, 34, 35.   [2] Acts xxii, 22.

"Ye have heard that it hath been said ... but I say unto you." Whenever this is done, it is not the act merely, but the evil thought or desire with respect to our brother that is forbidden. In every case it is the very spirit of the law which is to be carried out absolutely without restriction, and we must not think an evil thing with respect to our brother. "Ye have heard that it was said by them of old time, Thou shalt not kill; and whosoever shall kill shall be in danger of the judgment: but I say unto you, That whosoever is angry with his brother without a cause shall be in danger of the judgment: and whosoever shall say to his brother, Raca, shall be in danger of the council: but whosoever shall say, Thou fool, shall be in danger of hell fire."[1]

As in our day, so in the time of Christ, men found all sorts of pretexts to justify themselves in disobedience to the social law, and then, as now, one of the most frequent seems to have been gifts to further the maintenance of religious worship. It was thus that evil persons justified themselves for neglecting so plain a duty as the obligation to contribute to the support, when needful, of one's parents. If one said of money which ought to have been given to a father or mother, "It is corban," a gift for a religious

[1] Matthew v, 21, 22.

The Old and New Testaments. 65

establishment, then he was held to be under no obligation to minister to his parents. But Christ sternly rebuked those who maintained this tradition, and said unto them, that thus they had made the law of God of no effect. Christ mentions one duty after another to our fellows: love, forgiveness, etc.; and closes with, "Be ye therefore perfect, even as your Father which is in heaven is perfect."[1]

The intension of ethical obligation, as well as its extension, is illustrated by the emphasis laid on sins of omission. This is what the parable of Dives and Lazarus means. The writer well remembers a powerful sermon on this subject.[2] The message of the divine was a plain, simple one. We were asked, What was the offense of Dives? We have no reason to suppose that he was not respectable, was not a pillar of society, giving employment to many—and all that sort of thing. If we adhere to the Bible narrative—and we have no right to do anything else—the only fault we can find with him is that he did not think. He did not consider the poor; he passed by absorbed in his own concerns; he did not know the needs of the beggar at his gates; and so, we are told, he went to hell.

The same emphasis on omission is brought out

[1] Matthew v, 48.
[2] Preached by Bishop I. L. Nicholson, of Milwaukee, Wis.

in the account of the last judgment: Those who were sent away accursed are very much surprised when they are told by the Great Judge, "I was an hungered, and ye gave Me no meat: I was thirsty, and ye gave Me no drink: I was a stranger, and ye took Me not in: naked, and ye clothed Me not: sick, and in prison, and ye visited Me not." In their astonishment they ask, "When saw we Thee an hungered, or athirst, or a stranger, or naked, or sick, or in prison, and did not minister unto Thee?"[1] But they are told that their sin was one of omission; they had not done it to the least of the needy, and so they had not done it to the Judge. The same emphasis on omission is given by St. James in his epistle, "Therefore to him that knoweth to do good, and doeth it not, to him it is sin."[2]

St. Luke gives the spirit of Christ's entire mission in the sermon of Christ's which he records early in his gospel: "The Spirit of the Lord is upon me, because He hath anointed Me to preach the Gospel to the poor; He hath sent Me to heal the broken hearted, to preach deliverance to the captives, and recovering of sight to the blind, to set at liberty them that are bruised, to preach the acceptable year of the Lord."[3] This to be understood must be brought into immediate connection with the Year of Jubilee, to which it re-

[1] Matthew xxv, 31–46. [2] James iv, 17. [3] Luke, iv, 18, 19.

ferred. What was the purpose of the Year of Jubilee? Manifestly it had a social purpose; it aimed to abolish poverty, to secure as nearly as practicable a competency for all, to prevent vast accumulations, and generally to establish right relations among men. Had Christ's meaning been purely transcendental, referring to things of another world entirely, He would have had to explain himself to the Jews, whose hope was for righteousness in this world. He evidently wished them to think of the Year of Jubilee, and they were pleased with His message, "And all bare Him witness and wondered at the gracious words which proceeded out of His mouth."[1]

Take again the doctrine of stewardship. Unfortunately this doctrine gives satisfaction in proportion as it is vague and general; but, as taught in the New Testament, it is definite and precise enough. It has direct reference to the relations of Israel to the land which the nation held. This land was not the property of the nation, not even of the family, much less of the individual. It was God's property, and was assigned to families for their use under national regulation. It was literally a trust. And it was this trust which Christ extended and intensified.

Does not all this help us to understand better what the apparently contradictory statements in

[1] Luke iv, 22.

regard to the law of Moses mean? When the abolition of the law is spoken of, or is advocated, either in theory or practice, by Christ and His apostles, we have to do with the ceremonial law which separated the Jewish nation from other nations. This law had to pass away precisely because it was a wall of separation; but the social law could not pass away, not even one "jot or tittle," until all was fulfilled; on the contrary, that was extended to all the world, and intensified even to perfection.

Another thing must be noticed. Moses said nothing about a future life; his purpose was to establish the right relations among men in this world. He was well acquainted with the doctrine of the future life, and thus with the workings in Egypt of a religious system which had reference to the life to come, rather than the present. It has been held, and as the writer believes truly, that it is a strong proof of the divine character of the Old Testament that it is confined to the present world. Christ takes, undoubtedly, a step in advance. He brings to light and establishes conclusively, for all Christians, the doctrine of the resurrection and immortality; in short, eternal life. But, note: This eternal life begins in this world. The establishment of right relations in this world is our work, and is our preparation for the life to come. Again and again, when Christ's disciples would peer curiously into the future, they are turned aside to the present life and its duties. Christ thus kept in the footsteps of Moses, and His message was simply a further evolution of the teachings of Moses. His prayer says nothing about the future life, but teaches us to pray, "Thy Kingdom come, Thy will be done on earth as it is in Heaven."

"But," it may be objected, "did not Christ say in so many words, that His kingdom was not of this world?" Yes, truly. But the interpretation of these words cannot be extremely difficult when an attempt is made to interpret them in harmony with the other sayings of Christ and with the general spirit of His utterances. The world is frequently used to denote age or dispensation, and when we find the word "world" in the Bible we shall often catch the true idea involved if we substitute the word "age." Thus, whether we say, "the present wicked world," or "the present wicked age," is frequently immaterial. But more than this may be said. The world which is condemned, and which is the exact opposite of Christ's kingdom, is the world used in the sense of worldliness, and worldliness is essentially self-seeking, self-indulgence, and neglect of one's highest interests, as well as the welfare of others. When one condemns the worldly man or the worldly woman, one does not imply of necessity any doubt as to the ultimate triumph of Christ. We say of the worldly person, and of the saint of God, "They live in two different worlds." It is very true; Christ's kingdom is the direct antithesis of the one world, while the other world is that kingdom. The world in the bad sense is, indeed, defined in the First Epistle General of John as "the lust of the flesh, and the lust of the eyes, and the pride of life."[1] Yes, it is true; Christ's kingdom was not of the world which surrounded Him, nor is it of the world which envelops us; but our world is much nearer His coming kingdom. Things are becoming new, old things are passing away, and it is for Christ's people to make of the kingdoms of this world Christ's kingdom.

Finally, a few words must be devoted to the removal of misconceptions. We should remember, however, first of all in this connection, that it is infidels rather than Christians who interpret

---

[1] The Revised Version reads: "Vainglory of life" (1 John ii, 16).

Somewhat, but not precisely, the same idea is expressed in the following quotation: "The artificial, conventional order which communities establish among themselves—an order unnatural, transitory, and tending to corruption—has been called World, and has been contrasted by poets with Nature and by theologians with God."—Sir J. R. Seeley, *Natural Religion*, p. 83.

The Old and New Testaments. 71

Christ as one standing aloof from this world and its concerns, and directing the attention of men to the future life. If we would fairly understand Christ's preaching and conduct, we must remember He was a member of a subjugated nation. He was a Jew, living under the Roman power, and one teaching obedience to the civil authorities, paying tribute to Cæsar, and obeying the laws of Rome. When this is borne in mind, we must be more and more astonished at the social character of Christ's message. Naturally it was not what it would have been had the Jewish nation at that time been an independent sovereign nation. To understand the position of Christ, we must call before our mind the position of missionaries in foreign lands—let us say, Turkey in Asia. Now, missionaries in a land like Turkey, however much they may believe in social Christianity, must confine themselves exclusively to individual work; no other course is open to them. This individual work must, they believe, sooner or later, have its social consequences, and these missionaries must all regret the limitations that are imposed upon them; yet Christ went much further than any missionary—say, to Armenia in Turkey—will go to-day. He spoke continually of a kingdom, and this kingdom, however established, means a social organization. The establishment of this kingdom was the supreme thing with Christ. His enemies knew very well that this was a social message, and He knew it; but He adhered to His social message and laid down His life for it.

It can scarcely be necessary to go into verse after verse which is misinterpreted and often used as a support to those who would evade social responsibility. "Render unto Cæsar the things that are Cæsar's, and unto God the things that are God's;" this is an injunction of loyalty even to a foreign power which had conquered the nation. It recognized the sovereign authority although established by conquest. It is wrenching and twisting things out of all their connection to make this precept of Christ's imply an injunction on the part of Christians to neglect the affair of this world. The whole spirit of the Old and the New Testaments teaches us that we must strive for national righteousness and help to carry out God's purpose, which is to make the kingdoms of this world God's kingdoms.

Similarly Christ laid down principles which, carried out, will establish right relations among men. These right relations will be political, economic, social. The distribution of wealth will no more escape regulation in accordance with the principles of mutual love than any other social relation. But Christ refused, we

The Old and New Testaments. 73

hear it said, to divide the inheritance between two brothers when requested to do so by one of them.

Those who wish to draw from this a general principle in accordance with which Christianity has no concern with the distribution of wealth, should ask themselves what would have been the result if Christ, Himself, had undertaken to decide individual cases. First of all, we may observe that He would have had no time or energy for anything else. Second, we may notice that He would have come into conflict with the civil authorities. What Christ did was to lay down general principles to be carried out in detail by His followers in all generations to come. He laid down principles by which men were to settle their controversies, and His followers developed institutions which had in mind the regulation of economic and all other social relations, and these they carried out as far as the circumstances of the time permitted.

We thus see that the Gospel of Christ was an extension and intension of the teachings of the law and the prophets, and veritably "good tidings of great joy" for all the nations of the world, "from the rising of the sun, even unto the going down of the same."

CHAPTER IV.

THE SOCIAL LAW OF SERVICE.

"THEREFORE come what may, hold fast to love. Though men should rend your heart, let them not embitter or harden it. We win by tenderness, we conquer by forgiveness. O! strive to enter into something of that large celestial charity which is meek, enduring, unretaliating, and which even the overbearing world cannot withstand forever. Learn the new commandment of the Son of God. Not to love merely, but to love *as He loved*. Go forth in this spirit to your life duties; go forth, children of the Cross, to carry everything before you, and win victories for God by the conquering power of a love like his."—*Rev. Frederick W. Robertson, Sermons, p.* 184.

CHAPTER IV.

THE SOCIAL LAW OF SERVICE.

WE all crave happiness. Happiness is an end of life which is worthy of effort, but it is an end which must be subordinated to another end if it is to be pursued successfully; and this other end is service. But service means sacrifice; apparently the opposite of happiness. We reach this paradox then: Happiness is a worthy end of our efforts; but if we place it before ourselves as the direct and immediate end to be striven for, we cannot reach it. It will elude us. It will be to us like the water all about Tantalus, the cold flood welling ever to his chin, yet always retreating from his fiery lips; like the fruit over his head which the winds whirled skyward through the air:

"Whensoe'er,
 The old man fain to cool his burning tongue,
 Clutched with his fingers at the branches fair."

Individual lives repeat the race-history. If you would attain to happiness seek something else. Poets, philosophers, and prophets, all tell us this, for to all it comes as the result of the deepest insight and the ripest experience. But all go further. You must cast aside the thought of happiness as a chief aim. You may not keep it concealed in a corner of your mind and heart as after all the main thing, but a thing to be reached in a round-about way. You cannot successfully juggle with yourself. You must in very truth renounce yourself to find yourself, and give up yourself to save yourself.

To the author's mind there are few more interesting, more instructive, and withal pathetic life histories than that of John Stuart Mill, penned by himself. It is the story of a rarely gifted, noble nature, purposely brought up outside of the pale of Christianity and taught to look upon all religions as so many forms of superstition, yet gradually approaching the light as the years passed by. Mill tells us that in his early life his object was to be a reformer of the world, and that his conception of his own happiness was entirely identified with this object. He thought he had the certainty of a happy life, because he had placed his happiness in something durable and distant; in a goal toward which approach could always be made although it could never be reached. But Mill found that even so noble a pursuit could not give permanent happiness when happiness was the end sought. He reached a period when existence seemed almost an intoler-

The Social Law of Service. 79

able burden; a burden which he himself said was well described by Coleridge's lines on "Dejection:"

> "A grief without a pang, void, dark, and drear,
> A drowsy, stifled, unimpassioned grief,
> Which finds no natural outlet or relief,
> In word, or sigh, or tear."

When a moderate happiness returned he discovered that, "Those only are happy who have their mind fixed on some object other than their own happiness; as, the happiness of others, on the improvement of mankind, even on some art or pursuit, followed not as a means, but as itself an ideal end. Aiming thus at something else they find happiness by the way."

We have in these words of Mill a partial statement, at least, of the great ethical *law of indirectness*. We reach ethical ends only indirectly. Resolving to be good will in itself never make us good.

But shall we heap paradox on paradox? We have already found that while the craving for happiness is natural and the desire for happiness is legitimate, we shall lose it if we seek it. We have discovered that the secret of life is renunciation. We must sacrifice our life to receive it in fullness. "Surely, then, self-sacrifice is an end," we may be told. By no means. Self-sacrifice in itself is no virtue and may not be made an end in itself. Self-sacrifice pursued as an end leads to a gloomy asceticism which would have us refuse the joy of life as something bad and hateful to the Giver of all good things. Self-sacrifice bears its fruit of peace and happiness, and life only when it is pursued indirectly.

Self-sacrifice itself falls under the law of indirectness. `Let us listen to wise words of Bishop Boyd Carpenter: "A man cannot perfect himself in anything if he seek perfection directly; for, if he does, the shadow of himself intervenes and spoils his work. Sacrifice, when it is sought as a sacrifice, has a self-consciousness which mars its simplicity and spoils its moral force. When men preach self-sacrifice—self-sacrifice as the moral force which can regenerate mankind—they forget that self-forgetfulness is essential to perfect sacrifice; a sacrifice, undertaken because sacrifice is noble, is alloyed with that self-regarding look which mars its beauty in the view of the soul itself. Sacrifice which knows itself as such is not pure sacrifice."[1]

Have we not seen this in those who have found the secret of life? Have we not noticed how those whose life is wholly given to others—perhaps in some far-away land, deprived of almost everything which we hold dear—speak of their

[1] *The Permanent Elements of Religion*, pp. 36, 37.

privileges? Have we never heard a noble woman, wholly given to good works in a dreary slum of a great city, and who in the opinion of a host of admiring friends is almost ready for canonization, resent the thought that her life was one of self-sacrifice? Undoubtedly. And there is one word that gives the key to these paradoxes. What is it? We know what it is: Love—love, the secret of the universe. Sacrifice is not an end in itself, but sacrifice is the condition of service. The law of society is service. This is the supreme law of society from which no one can escape with impunity. Ethical teachers now approach unanimity in the assertion that the criterion of right conduct is social well-being. The welfare of society is the test of conduct in the individual. It would be interesting to take four great writers—a theologian, a jurist, a professor of natural science, and a student of society —and to discover their entire and complete harmony in the view that the purpose of the rules of right individual conduct is the welfare of society.

There is one law, and only one, taught by the Christian religion and on its manward side; that is, the law of love, which finds expression in the social law of service. Christianity and ethical science agree perfectly. Social welfare is the test of right conduct. All right laws which regulate human relations have in view the well-being of society and they are all one. Thus it is true that he who breaks any one law breaks all, for they all have one source and one purpose. The thief and the undutiful child, the murderer and the slothful person, all alike have violated the social law of service. When you utter unkind words, when you neglect an opportunity to lend a helping hand, when you spend material wealth to gratify whim, caprice, vanity, instead of to accomplish worthy ends, you have broken the same law which has been violated by the criminal classes in our prisons and penitentiaries.

This may seem like a hard saying, but the more we ponder it, the more meaning it will have for us. And the message which it conveys to us is one which is needed in these days of great wealth and easy-going self-indulgence, if it ever was needed.

It will be well for us to contrast at some length Christian self-sacrifice, the condition of social service with asceticism, which is its perversion. The two following quotations will be so helpful to us that we take them as a text in our treatment of the entire subject of Christian self-sacrifice *versus* asceticism:

"Then said Jesus unto His disciples, If any man will come after Me, let him deny himself, and take up his cross, and follow Me.

"For whosoever will save his life shall lose it: and whosoever will lose his life for my sake shall find it."[1]

"The first condition of all really great moral excellence is a spirit of genuine self-sacrifice and self-renunciation."[2]

An enduring truth is expressed in these quotations. The first is one of these pregnant sayings of Christ which have been bearing fruit for nearly two thousand years, and which are as vital to-day in Christendom as ever before. They have, indeed, but begun to do their work, because they contain lessons founded on the fundamental principles of man's nature. They belong to no age and to no country. They reveal that marvelous insight, not merely into human nature, but into the depths of moral and spiritual truth, which again and again has provoked from men the spontaneous and surprised exclamation: "Never man spake like this man."[3] What Emerson says—with some exaggeration, perhaps—of Plato, is fully true of Christ in the sense in which Emerson uses the words: "The citizen of an Eastern [Greek] town, but no villager nor patriot." Christ was one of those who, in the best sense of the word, are cosmopolitan—belonging to the

---

[1] Matthew xvi, 24, 25.
[2] Lecky, *History of European Morals*, ii, 155.
[3] John vii, 46.

world—laying the foundations of a true patriotism, yet not patriotic in a narrow and exclusive sense, because transcending all national bounds.

The second quotation, taken from Lecky's *History of European Morals*, is the author's profound reflection after his admirable study of Christian asceticism, and is, perhaps, all the more significant because the author reaches his conclusions as a result, not of religious experiences, but of independent investigations and historical researches.

What is the difference between Christian self-sacrifice and asceticism? Certainly it is not in the degree of self-renunciation. What asceticism has exacted from those who have thought to find in it the way of life, we may read in the painful narrative of Lecky. Wife, husband, children, the blessings of civilization enjoyed in the midst of abundant comfort, pleasures of every sort, all have been exchanged gladly for the hermit's cell, often a wild beast's den in the desert, for rags and filth, for the scantiest diet, for long vigils, for castigations, for privations and sufferings, which have cut short thousands of lives. St. Simeon Stylites, on his pillar, bidding his attendant replace the worms which fed on his flesh, as they fell from the sickening sores of his disgusting body, saying to the worms, " Eat what God has given you," is a well-known type of the

The Social Law of Service. 85

ascetic. Blaise Pascal is one of the higher types of the ascetic, and his self-inflicted tortures are described in these words: " To avoid wandering and worldly thoughts when engaged in conversation, he took an iron girdle full of sharp points, which he placed next to his flesh, and when conscious of an impulse to vanity, or even a feeling of pleasure in the place where he happened to be, he struck the girdle with his elbow in order to increase the pain of the punctures. He ate a certain regulated quantity of food whether hungry or not, never exceeding it, however good his appetite, and never eating less, however great his loathing; and this on the ground that taking food was a duty, which was never to be accompanied by any sensual pleasure. . . . He mortified his affections not less than his body, and said that we should never allow anyone to love us with fondness; in fostering such attachments we occupied hearts which ought to be given solely to God; that it was robbing Him of that on which He set most store. 'It is not right that others should attach themselves to me, even if they do it willingly and with pleasure. I should deceive those in whom I excited such a feeling. Am I not about to die? The object of their love will then perish. As I should warn people against believing a falsehood, however profitable to me, I should warn them not to attach themselves to me; for their duty is to spend their lives in striving to please God, or in seeking Him.'"[1]

Yet the sufferings of the ascetic were not more severe than those which Christ invited His followers to endure. How strange the allurements held out to men to join the Christian ranks in the time of Christ and His apostles! The birds of the air have their nests, the beasts of the field have their holes, but I, the Christ, have nowhere to lay My head, yet follow Me. I am not to receive earthly honors, as has been vainly supposed—I shall be despised and rejected, persecuted to the death, hung upon the shameful cross to die an ignominious death, yet follow Me and see the things which I must suffer. Do not think, however, that you will fare better than I! Far from it. If they have called me Beelzebub, how much more shall they call you the children of hell! If I have been maltreated, so shall you also be scourged, imprisoned, crucified. Follow Me and I will show you how great things you must suffer for Me! Did ever captain draw his hosts about him with such promise of reward? Yet a response to the call of Christ has never been lacking. From the time of Christ to this day an interesting multitude of believers have accepted the call to suffer

---

[1] J. C. Morison, *Service of Man*, pp. 211, 212.

The Social Law of Service. 87

for Christ, and accepted it not only without reservation but with joy. Remember the conversion of St. Paul. The disciple of Christ who hesitated to receive the persecuting Saul is reassured with these words: "He is a chosen vessel unto Me, ... for I will show him how great things he must suffer for My name's sake." And St. Paul entered on his work, not with assurances of great success in a large field of usefulness, not with promises of large victories as a result of battles with the enemies of Christ, but with the knowledge that he must bear unusual cruelties. This was his incitement, this was the inducement held out for an alliance with a despised sect. Yet gladly did St. Paul accept the proffer, and before the end of his sufferings we find him describing with a certain feeling of exultation his experiences as a follower of the Nazarene: "Of the Jews five times received I forty stripes save one. Thrice was I beaten with rods, once was I stoned, thrice I suffered shipwreck, a night and a day I have been in the deep; in journeyings often, in perils of waters, in perils of robbers, in perils by mine own countrymen, in perils by the heathen, in perils in the city, in perils in the wilderness, in perils in the sea, in perils among false brethren; in weariness and painfulness, in watchings often, in hunger and thirst, in fastings often, in cold and nakedness; besides those things that are without, there is that which presseth upon me daily, anxiety for all the churches."[1],[2]

Nevertheless there is a marked difference between the exhortations of Christ and the entreaties of the preachers of ascetism and self-renunciation. Asceticism is self-denial for its own sake, and Christ never urged that upon His followers. What the world offers is in itself good and to be enjoyed with thanksgiving. The flowers of the field have been clothed by God with a beauty of which Solomon could not boast, to rejoice the eye of man. The beasts and fields produce food and raiment in abundance, and all innocent enjoyment is a positive duty rather than a sin. Rejoice and be exceeding glad for the gifts of your heavenly Father; this is the spirit of Christ.

We may, indeed, rejoice that we have been emancipated from the bonds of a gloomy asceticism which made a virtue of sacrifice and suffering in themselves. Suffering goes with sin; joy with righteousness. Christ came to make this world a happy world and, as His purposes approach completion, happiness of the highest sort

---

[1] 2 Corinthians xi, 24-28.
[2] The author wishes to acknowledge at this point the valuable assistance received from Bishop Boyd Carpenter's *Permanent Element of Religion*, from which book this illustration and some other quotations are taken.

The Social Law of Service. 89

must increase. This world will become a happier and happier world as time goes on, for the coming of the kingdom means the subjugation of the entire world to Christ. And by the entire world we understand not only man, but external physical forces. This thought is clearly revealed in the prophecies of the Old Testament, especially in Isaiah: "Instead of the thorn shall come up the fir tree, and instead of the brier shall come up the myrtle tree."[1] This signifies the subjugation of the forces of nature, but nature includes man's physical body, and that, too, in a righteous state, will have long life gradually, peacefully, fading away at last. "And I will rejoice in Jerusalem, and joy in my people: and the voice of weeping shall be no more heard in her, nor the voice of crying. There shall be no more thence an infant of days, nor an old man that hath not filled his days: for the child shall die an hundred years old. . . . They shall build houses, and inhabit them; and they shall plant vineyards, and eat the fruit of them. . . . For as the days of a tree are the days of my people, and mine elect shall long enjoy the work of their hands."[2]

The miracles of Christ have this same significance. The Son of man must show Himself Lord of the external physical world in order to bring out its significance and the ultimate domi-

[1] Isaiah lv, 13.   [2] Isaiah lxv, 19-22.

nation of man. The miracles puzzle many, but when we think about it in this light we must see that the life of the Messiah would have been strangely incomplete without them. This must be felt by all who think deeply on social righteousness and its results. The teachings of the French socialist, Fourier, are instructive at this point. These teachings are wild and erratic in many particulars. They contain much chaff, but in the chaff we find valuable grains of wheat. Fourier predicted a happy social state to continue long in the future, and he prophesied that in this state lions should become servitors of man, drawing his chariot hundreds of miles in a single day, that whales should draw his ships across the great deep, while the ocean itself would become a delightful beverage.[1]

We laugh at these crude fantasies, yet there is in them the sound thought indicated.

But we have in all this only the teachings of history and the revelations of natural science. National wickedness has repeatedly turned fruitful plains into deserts and social righteousness is capable of turning barren wastes once more into smiling gardens.

Yet there is the great fact of self-denial and self-renunciation—" the first condition of all really great moral excellence." And this fact,

[1] Ely, *French and German Socialism*, pp. 88, 89.

The Social Law of Service. 91

stern and unrelenting, so far from anywhere in the New Testament being concealed, is thrust —at times it would seem almost with unnatural violence—into the foreground of the entire Gospel message.

Why did Christ Himself suffer? Why was He, although keenly appreciative of the beauties of nature and social in His disposition, loving to eat and drink with His friends—why was He "a man of sorrows and acquainted with grief?"[1] These words contain the explanation: "And I, if I be lifted up, will draw all men unto Me." Ah, the sacrifice of Christ had an object outside of Himself. It was not sacrifice for sacrifice' sake, but sacrifice for others' sake. Because Christ loved men with an infinite yearning love, He died for men. Love was the ground of sacrifice. "God is love." This is the secret of Christian self-denial, and asceticism, whatever its external resemblance, is its perversion. It is like the perversion of charity, in the lower sense of the word charity; that is to say, almsgiving. Men first gave to benefit their fellows, then later, in the time of the perversion, to benefit themselves by accumulating thereby, as it was supposed, heavenly treasures; but when the true end

---

[1] Those persons who think they imitate Christ in merely wearing long faces, miss the mark widely. It was the intense sympathy of Christ which made Him sad.

of charity was lost sight of, it became a curse and not a blessing to the world. It is not said that a proper motive in giving is not the benefit which may come to one's character, but a true saint will scarcely think of this, but only of those to whom he hopes to minister, because he loves them as children of a common Father. The self-motive is altogether subordinate. Likewise it is not claimed that self-denial should not be practiced for the sake of character-culture, and we may admit an educational value in asceticism, though we claim the same end can otherwise be reached and that by methods more in harmony with the teachings of Christ.

Asceticism, indeed, often grows out of self-sacrifice. Men go without for the sake of others; then, later, they lose their love for others and continue their self-denial as if there were virtue in that of itself. The spirit is gone, the lifeless form alone remains. Thus asceticism has often displaced love to others and become intensely cruel.

Love leads to self-sacrifice of necessity, as we see in the lives of those who have manifested in a marked degree generous love for men. The biography of the seventh Earl of Shaftesbury shows us this; also, the biography of two American women, the Grimké sisters.[1] These sisters

[1] *The Sisters Grimké*, a Biography, by Catherine H. Birney.

illustrated the motto on the title-page of the book in which is recorded the story of their lives: "The glory of all glories is the glory of self-sacrifice." At first sacrifice with them found a basis in asceticism. It was thought well pleasing to God that they should deny themselves without any human motive or aim external to themselves. This early period of their history finds expression in many passages in the book. Sarah Grimké writes: "I went to meeting, and it being a rainy day I took a large, handsome umbrella which I had accepted from brother Henry, accepted doubtfully, therefore wrongfully, and have never felt quite easy to use it, which, however, I have done a few times. After I was in meeting I was much tried by a wandering mind, and every now and then the umbrella would come before me, so that I sat trying to wait on my God, and He showed me that I must not only give up this little thing, but return it to my brother." After other reflections she adds, in a note: "This little sacrifice was made. I sent the umbrella with an affectionate note to brother, and believe it gave him no offense to have it returned, and sweet has been the recompense, even peace."

Angelina says: "A great deal of my finery, too, I have put beyond the reach of anyone." She had put into a cushion two handsome lace

veils, a lace flounce, and other laces. This was
done, as she wrote on a slip of paper sewed up in
the cushion, " under feelings of duty, believing
that as we are called with a high and holy
calling, and forbidden to adorn these bodies, but
to wear the ornament of a meek and quiet
spirit, as we have ourselves laid (in this cushion)
these superfluities of naughtiness, so we should
not in any measure contribute to the destroying
of others;" that is, by allowing others to wear
all this finery. The sisters wanted at this time
by such means to separate themselves from the
world and condemn it. Angelina was troubled
by a cashmere mantle which had cost a sum
which then seemed large to her, and cut the
trimming off; but this did not suit her, and she
finally decided never to wear it again although
she had at the time no money to replace it with
anything else.

Soon, however, we perceive other motives,
motives of an altruistic nature, appearing as the
ground of self-sacrifice. Angelina writes in her
diary at a somewhat later date than the time of
the last quotation: " It is not only the food I
eat at mother's, but the whole style of living is a
direct departure from the simplicity that is in
Christ. The Lord's poor tell me that they do
not like to come to such a fine house to see me;
and if they come, instead of reading a lesson of

frugality and deadness to the world, they must go away lamenting the inconsistency of a sister professor. One thing is very hard to bear. I feel obliged to pay five dollars a week for board [then a much larger sum than now], though I disapprove of this extravagance, and am actually accessory in maintaining this style of living, and am therefore prevented from giving to the poor as liberally as I would like."

It was not, however, until these sisters were aroused to the wrong of slavery, and began to take a part in the abolition movement, that the full measure of their capabilities for self-sacrifice appeared, and then self-sacrifice found its true basis in love for others. They lived a life of self-sacrifice then because, loving others and perceiving the needs of others, they could not do otherwise. They with all their resources were dedicated to what they deemed a holy cause, and every cent saved from personal expenditure was a cent to be used to help others. They had, indeed, a "love-purse," as it was called, into which such savings were dropped. These sisters Grimké were the daughters of Judge Grimké, of Charleston, S. C., and were brought up like young ladies in the best Southern social circles. Only those who know what this means can appreciate the self-sacrifice in them when they lived in a rude little cottage in New Jersey, across the Hudson from

New York, and did their own housework, dressing simply, while the husband of one of the sisters, Theodore Weld, wore noticeably coarse clothing, which he thought might have cost him nearly one hundred dollars one year, when he was traveling and lecturing, and the whole of one suit and part of another were destroyed by mobs. Listen to a few quotations from letters. Sarah writes: " We can make good bread, and this with milk is an excellent meal. This week I am cook, and am writing this while my beans are boiling and pears stewing for dinner." Angelina writes at another time : " As to how I have made out with cooking, it so happens that labor (planting a garden) gives Theodore such an appetite that everything is sweet to him, so that my rice and asparagus, potatoes, mush, and Indian bread, all taste well, though some might not think them fit to eat." Shortly after her marriage to Mr. Weld, Angelina wrote: " We ordered our furniture to be made of cherry, and quite enjoy the cheapness of our outfit, for the less we spend the less the Antislavery Society will have to pay my Theodore for his labors."

Does it not become apparent that this represents the spirit which must of necessity animate all Christians? No one can love his fellows truly and waste any resources.

Now this parallel between charity and asceticism, to which allusion has already been made, is instructive in another sense. Men saw the evils connected with perverted charity, and said: "Charity is a bad thing. Gifts are bad things. One may sell things, but may not without injury give them away. Self-seeking is a beneficent social law." Thus men substitute the teachings of Satan for the commands of Christ. Without love we may not, it is true, give to our fellows and benefit them.

Likewise in our day men, perceiving the excesses of asceticism, and the cruel selfishness which has too often accompanied it, and even been a part of it, have acquiesced silently or openly in self-indulgence. Give nothing without a valuable equivalent, and enjoy all that your resources permit you to enjoy—this is the logical conclusion of much that passes for Christian teaching.

No earnest man is to-day satisfied with the influence of the Christian Church. Its members are not leading the life which is expected of them. It may or may not be true that they are better than they have been in former ages, but we are still sadly far behind the mark. Under present circumstances what is particularly needed is for us to take home to ourselves the doctrine of Christian self-sacrifice. To renounce "the devil and all his works, the vain pomp and glory of the world, with all covetous desires of the same, and the sinful desires of the flesh, so as not to follow or be led by them," is a very real thing and a very great sacrifice. It is a cross which only the love of Christ can make an easy burden. Our resources of every sort, time, strength of body and mind, and our economic resources, are all limited, and, however great they may be, love will show us how we can use all to the last minute of time and the last farthing of money for the promotion of the welfare of humanity.

Let us consider a few quotations from great thinkers who are strongly impressed with the necessity of self-sacrifice, and the testimony for present purposes is perhaps all the more valuable because so many of them profess slight allegiance to Christianity. Says Carlyle: "It is only with renunciations that life properly speaking can be said to begin."[1] . . .

"In a valiant suffering for others, not in a slothful making others suffer for us, did nobleness ever lie."[2]

George Sand uses these words: "There is only one sole virtue in the world—the eternal sacrifice of self."

---

[1] *Sartor Resartus*, quoted by Bishop Boyd Carpenter in his *Permanent Element of Religion*, pp. 350, 351.
[2] *Past and Present.*

The Social Law of Service. 99

George Eliot sings:
"May I reach
That purest heaven; be to other souls
The cup of strength in some great agony.
 . . . .
So shall I join the choir invisible,
Whose music is the gladness of the world."

Another writer[1] expresses himself as follows: "You talk of self as the motive to exertion; I tell you it is the abnegation of self which has wrought out all that is noble, all that is good, all that is useful, nearly all that is ornamental, in the world."

Our American philosopher, Emerson, says: "A man was born, not for prosperity, but to suffer for the benefit of others, like the noble rock-maple, which all round our villages bleeds for the service of man."[2]

Let us hear the great German, the poet Goethe: "Everything cries out to us that we must renounce. Thou must go without, go without! That is the everlasting song which every hour, all our life through, hoarsely sings to us: Die, and come to life; for so long as this is not accomplished thou art but a troubled guest upon an earth of gloom."[3]

Matthew Arnold, from whom these last quota-

[1] Whyte Melville, *Bones and I.*
[2] Emerson, *Method of Nature.*
[3] M. Arnold, *Literature and Dogma*, pp. 186, 187.

tions are taken, expounds these words of Jesus: "He that loveth his life shall lose it; and he that hateth his life in this world shall keep it unto life eternal." "Whosoever will come after Me, let him renounce himself, and take up his cross daily, and follow Me." He tells us that these words contain the secret of Jesus, and says: "Perhaps there is no other maxim of Jesus which has such a combined stress of evidence for it, and may be taken as so eminently His." This is the secret by which His Gospel, says Arnold, brought life and immortality to light, and it is repeated by each one of the four gospel writers.

The writer has often thought of a remark made by a principal of a Normal School in a New England State. This principal was a lady who had been brought up in the strict ways of a religious denomination which in her childhood was inclined to be severe in many of its requirements, but she had changed with the change of her church and had become liberal in her views. She asked one day, "Why is it that when I want a faithful teacher in my school, I seek a young woman brought up in the old strict ways in which I myself no longer believe?"

Do we not come, in what has been said, to the root of the difficulty? It is better for men to be called upon even by superstition and false religion to make self-sacrifice, than to lead a life of

The Social Law of Service. 101

self-indulgence; and a certain so-called liberalizing tendency in all the churches has been overinclined to say simply: Thou mayest do this, thou mayest do that; go to the theater, dance, play cards, enjoy a good horse race, etc. Now, if this teaching be true, it is only half of the truth. We need not now enter into the question of dancing, card playing, etc. If the reader objects to these, he will see an argument in what has been said for his convictions. If the reader regards these as innocent recreations, then he will, perhaps, be more keenly aware than before how near to their use is their abuse. If the old restrictions are removed, new ones equally, nay, more severe, are raised by the duty to love and serve our fellows, and to make of the earth God's kingdom.

A young lad, full of the enthusiasm of humanity and eager for self-sacrifice, once said: "Father, I almost feel sorry that slavery has been abolished, and that I can have no part in that struggle." Alas! evils still exist, evils as bad as slavery, and those who fight the world, the flesh, and the devil will still have opportunity to suffer. Frequently men will not speak well of them, but will turn them the cold shoulder, will malign, slander, and persecute them. Christ said to the men of His day: "Woe unto you! for ye build the sepulchers of the prophets, and your fathers killed them."[1] These words express a permanent historical truth. We are all brave with respect to the struggles of the past, and we honor the memory of those we would have helped to persecute had we lived in their day. When the twentieth century is well advanced, it may be found that we have been stoning those to whom our children will then be erecting monuments. The world advances, true, and in some respects it is easier to do good than before, but there is still no lack of opportunity to suffer. The cross is still a reality.

The Roman Catholic Church provides opportunities for self-renunciation the most complete. To Protestants this often appears worse than useless; but it is, nevertheless, one source of its strength. May not our own Protestant churches return from one of the mistakes of Protestantism, and in orders of deaconesses, brotherhoods, sisterhoods, and associations of lay worshipers provide a fruitful channel into which self-sacrificing efforts can flow to the glory of God and the good of our fellow-men? Let us, at any rate, see to it that for us religion is something more than a " graceful and pleasing appendix to life."

[1] Luke xi, 47.

CHAPTER V.

THE SOCIAL SIGNIFICANCE OF BAPTISM AND THE LORD'S SUPPER.

"It is to be noted, that whereas nothing in this life is more acceptable before God, or more pleasant unto man, than Christain people to live together quietly in love and peace, unity and concord, this sacrament doth most aptly and effectuously move us thereunto. For when we be made all partakers of this one table, what ought we to think, but that we be all members of one spiritual body, whereof Christ is the head; that we be joined together in one Christ, as a great number of grains of corn be joined together in one loaf? Surely, they have very hard and stony hearts, which with these things be not moved; and more cruel and unreasonable be they than brute beasts, that cannot be persuaded to be good to their Christian brethren and neighbors, for whom Christ suffered death, when in this sacrament they be put in remembrance that the Son of God bestowed His life for His enemies. For we see by daily experience, that eating and drinking together maketh friends, and continueth friendship; much more then ought the table of Christ to move us so to do."—*Archbishop Cranmer, on The Lord's Supper, Parker Society Publications, pp. 42, 43.*

CHAPTER V.

THE SOCIAL SIGNIFICANCE OF BAPTISM AND THE LORD'S SUPPER.

IT is a strange thing how we forget one half of the Gospel message, and precisely that half which Christ emphasized. We slur it over, and do not perceive its import when we read the Bible. Having eyes we see not, having ears we hear not, the true tests of Christianity. Herein is revealed the marvelous nature of Christianity. All religions exalt a superior being, or at any rate profess to exalt a superior being, but as we have already seen it is a distinctive feature of Christ's teaching that Man is exalted—man created a little lower than the angels—"a little lower than God," we are told is the correct translation.

The beloved Apostle John plunges into the heart of Christ's doctrine when he affirms, " If a man say, I love God, and hateth his brother, he is a liar: for he that loveth not his brother whom he hath seen, how can he love God whom he hath not seen?" St. Paul ventures to affirm, " The whole law is fulfilled in one word, even in this: Thou shalt love thy neighbor as thyself."

The first great commandment is not mentioned in this place by St. Paul, whereas Christ and his apostles nowhere sum up all the law without mentioning the second. It is as if the first were something assumed—something which could be assumed as a mere matter of course, but as if the second were something which needed perpetual emphasis, and must ever again and again be brought forward as the test of a Christ-life.

Such a view has been confirmed by the entire history of the Christian Church. Men have been ever ready to substitute alleged service to God for true service to man, and have employed a multitude of devices to reconcile cruelty and neglect of one's fellows with membership in the body of Christ. Vain effort! How painfully, in the great day of judgment which must come to every soul, will the veil pretense be torn away! "Lord, Lord," will many a one say—"Lord, Lord, have we not been zealous champions of orthodox creeds; have we not made long prayers; have we not attended the regular services of the church; have we not said our verses and told our experiences in our meetings; did we not lead Epworth Leagues and Societies of Christian Endeavor?" But then the neglected portions of the Gospel will come into the consciousness and burn like flames of fire—neglected portions, such as these: " Pure religion and undefiled before God and the

Father is this, To visit the fatherless and widows in their affliction, and to keep himself unspotted from the world." . . . " Therefore, to him that knoweth to do good "—to him that hath abundance and useth this abundance for himself, while neglected children die needlessly by the hundred thousand in the slums of the cities; to him that useth his resources for luxurious self-indulgence, while untold thousands of young people are growing up in our lands without wholesome physical, mental, and spiritual food, hurrying forward on the road to perdition; to him that exalted himself so above others that he spendeth his substance for superfluities while others lack the things necessary to worthy human life—"to him that knoweth to do good, but doeth it not, to him it is sin." And how will a passage like this one day burn into the souls of some who talk to us about the "simple Gospel of Christ," meaning thereby an emasculated gospel which extends only to public worship and not to the markets of the world, where they claim self-interest rightly reigns supreme : "Woe unto you, . . . for ye devour widows' houses, and for a pretense make long prayer: therefore ye shall receive the greater damnation?"

We have in this passage just quoted the condemnation of positive wrongdoing to our neighbor. But, as we have already seen, the severest words are reserved for simple neglect to serve our fellows in need: " I was an hungered, and ye gave me no meat."

The social side of Christianity is not something which may be neglected or not. The manward aspects of Christianity are an essential part of it—an essential part, without which it cannot exist. Some Christians speak, and most Christians act, as if philanthropy were a sort of ornamental appendage to Christianity, pleasing enough if it exists, but something apart from its very essence. And some, wiser than Christ, even claim this in so many words; but Christ and His apostles teach that philanthropy is more than a cloak; more than garments to protect; even more than food to nourish; that it is a part of the very being of Christianity.

Our poets and sages have often enough told us this, but we have viewed them with suspicion, and have been ready to bring charges of heresy against them when they have repeated to us Christ-words.

What does James Russell Lowell tell us?

" He's true to God who's true to man ; wherever wrong is done
To the humblest and the weakest 'neath the self-beholding sun,
That wrong is done to us."

Listen to Ruskin, who follows his condemnation, "You might sooner get lightning out of incense smoke than true action or passion out

Of Baptism and the Lord's Supper. 109

of your modern English religion," with this definition of a true Church: "Wherever one hand meets another helpfully, that is the holy mother Church which ever is or ever shall be."

Certainly no true definition of the Church can be less inclusive. A true definition of the Church may be more inclusive—doubtless is more inclusive—but not less conclusive.

The effect of dwelling chiefly on the theological and neglecting the social side of Christianity is observed in inadequate ideas touching Baptism and the Lord's Supper. Rarely is their social significance brought out, and it is not at present deeply impressed on the consciousness of the Christian Church. It is not a part of the ordinary and habitual thought of Christians respecting these sacraments. Yet their social significance is most marked. It is no new discovery, for it has been present in the minds and hearts of Christians as a mighty power. Even now it is not entirely forgotten, but it has rather, as it were, fallen out of the Christian consciousness of modern times; it has, if we may use the expression, become subconscious, and although now and again temporarily brought forward into the consciousness, it has lost its due relative importance for us. This social significance is fraternity.

A few words only will be said about Baptism,

and that for several reasons. One is that the social significance of the Lord's Supper is perhaps more marked; another, that Baptism is a topic which theological differences have made more difficult of treatment on its social side. But whatever views we hold respecting the significance of Baptism on its Godward side, it cannot be overlooked that it has its social meaning. It is the method whereby we enter into relations with our fellows and form the Church of Christ. "All one body we," but it is through the doorway of Baptism that we enter into the visible Church. All men are brothers, but among those thus connected there is a peculiarly closer relation. But the broader relations must not be overlooked. As has been well said by one valued highly by multitudes in all religious denominations: "Baptism is a visible witness to the world of that which the world is forever forgetting—a common humanity united in God. Baptism authoritatively reveals and pledges to the individual that which is true of the race."[1] The splendid declaration of solidarity in Christ which the Apostle Paul makes in the Epistle to the Galatians[2] is connected with baptism, although this is often overlooked: "For as many of you as have been baptized into Christ have

---

[1] Rev. F. W. Robertson, *Sermons*, p. 274.
[2] Galatians iii, 26 29.

put on Christ. There is neither Jew nor Greek, there is neither bond nor free, there is neither male nor female: for ye are all one in Christ Jesus."

And may we not for a moment turn our attention to infant baptism? For those who do not hold that baptism works a change in the infant baptized, has not the baptism of infants chiefly a social significance — a significance which is something added to its deeper meaning for those who accept the doctrine of baptismal regeneration? It would seem that here we have a common standing ground for all those who hold to infant baptism, and one which may render this institution more precious than it is now in the eyes of many. Infant baptism recalls the fact that Christ proposed a universal kingdom as successor to the national kingdom of the Jews, and that as circumcision was in a manner naturalization of the infant in the national kingdom, so baptism is in like manner naturalization in the universal kingdom. It points to the solidarity of the family in the kingdom of Christ, and recalls the fact that the first converts in Europe were families, namely, Lydia and her household, the jailer and all his. Like Joshua of old, the Christian father of a family in the baptism of his infant children proclaims to the world, "As for

[1] Bishop B. F. Westcott, *The Incarnation and Common Life.*

me and my house, we will serve the Lord."[1] Fortunately, the view of the kingdom of God enunciated in this book by no means depends upon infant baptism alone, for among those who on theological grounds reject this right are found many strong adherents of this conception of the kingdom, but it does give a richer and fuller significance to infant baptism for other Christians who have overlooked its import of solidarity in Christ.

Turning our attention to the Lord's Supper, we find the claim made that bread and wine, rather than other kinds of food and drink, were chosen by Christ because they typified fraternity so admirably; many grains of wheat but one loaf of bread, "for we being many are one bread," writes St. Paul; many grapes but one cup of wine. As Archbishop Cranmer says in the quaint language of his time: "For like as bread is made of a great number of grains of corn, ground, broken, and so joined together that thereof is made one loaf; and an infinite number of grapes be pressed together in one vessel, and thereof is made wine; likewise is the whole multitude of true Christian people spiritually joined, first to Christ, and then among themselves, together in one faith, one baptism, one Holy Spirit, one knot and bond of love."[2]

[1] Joshua xxiv, 15.
[2] Archbishop Cranmer on The Lord's Supper, p. 42.

Of Baptism and the Lord's Supper. 113

The Godward side of the Lord's Supper draws us to heaven, and bids us contemplate in humility the infinite yearning love of our Father revealed to us in our blessed Lord and Saviour, and so to receive the bread and wine in remembrance of His death and passion "that we may be partakers of His most blessed body and blood."[1]

The manward side of the Lord's Supper draws us to our fellows and bids us love men as Christ loved men, giving ourselves for them even to the extent of washing workingmen's feet in our passion for the service of man; bids us spend time and substance, strength of body and mental faculties, to seek and save the lost.

This manward side of the Lord's Supper when it becomes real will inspire Christians with ceaseless activity for the redemption of the world—and no less a task has Christ given them—and when exhausted by labor and long vigils they contemplate such sights as we can see in New York and Chicago, or in any other great town—ay, even in the country; ay, even in many a county jail, a veritable high school of crime—

---

[1] The writer has adhered to the form of the Ritual of the Methodist Episcopal Church. Other Christians may believe more than is implied in these words, but not less, and in a work of this kind it is desirable to avoid, so far as possible, even the appearance of theological differences.

they will in anguish repeat the words of Christ, the Infinite Love, "O Jerusalem, Jerusalem, . . . how often would I have gathered thy children together, even as a hen gathereth her chickens under her wings, but ye would not!"

When the Lord's table is spread, brothers and sisters in Christ partake of a common meal— eat from the same plate, drink out of the same cup—and this from most ancient times has been regarded both as symbolic of brotherhood and promotive of brotherhood.

To partake of one's salt, to break bread together, are terms of significance. The very savage either refuses to eat with his enemy, or first lays aside his enmity. The untamed and cruel Indian, as we have learned in many a noble and touching tale, is bound to him at whose table and with whom he has eaten.

To this day German students drink "Brüderschaft"—brotherhood. When with locked arms they drink together, they no longer use in addressing each, "Sie" (you), which is the common form of address among friends and acquaintances, but ever after they employ "Du" (thou), a term by which brothers and sisters and intimate friends address each other. Even after this single ceremony they make use of the terms of fraternity.

Notice, too, that the violation of this feeling of

Of Baptism and the Lord's Supper. 115

fraternity by Judas, one who sat at the same table with Him, seemed to add a new pang to our Saviour's woes: "He that eateth bread with me hath lifted up his heel against me."

The Germans have a term, "tafelfähig," worthy to sit at table (on state occasions at least). "Tafelfähig"—worthy to sit at the royal table—is a high distinction. It means a long line of distinguished ancestry, pure blood, or high service to the state. Sitting at the same table elevates one as it were to a fraternal relation with the host making them of one family. So among us who belong to the more ordinary humanity, those who sit at a common table, are, for the time being at least, in our social circle, even if not necessarily equal. But relative equality is the marked feature, and in the great world those with whom we cannot mingle as friends do not sit at table with us.

In the Lord's Supper we sit at the table of Him who is Lord of lords and King of kings, and among us human beings, weak and erring human beings, "miserable sinners," equality swallows up inequality. We, so far below Him in power and holiness, in our humility and penitence fail to recognize what must then appear to be insignificant differences. Let not the prince presume at this table to jostle and push the beggar. "My brother," "My sister," these words must at such a time be the natural mode of address. This mode of address undoubtedly arose spontaneously, but, continued in absence of a spirit of fraternity, became such a hollow mockery that generally even the pretense has been dropped,[1] and too often nothing distinguishes the cold formality of Christians partaking of a common meal from that of worldly gatherings. Some way or another, whatever progress has been made in other respects, there has been sad retrogression in this vital matter of fraternity, when we compare the present with certain earlier periods, although now we may be—God grant it!—again advancing in Christ-life when we compare the present with a nearer past.

Yet, what can be more disheartening than the use of individual communion cups here and there? Is not the meaning of the Lord's Supper thereby half lost? Indeed, may we not say that to the worldly-minded this innovation must seem like a caricature of the sacrament? The loving-cup still passes from mouth to mouth in many a social gathering in every land, and signifies fraternity outside the church, but within the church hundreds of little glasses on huge trays are carried

---

[1] Perhaps the practice is continued more generally in some religious denominations than others; and doubtless is more frequent in smaller towns than in the great cities; doubtless also more common among poor than among wealthy Christians.

Of Baptism and the Lord's Supper. 117

about, or other new devices are employed to avoid what is after all little more than an imaginary danger. And if, after all, in this service of Christ, one soldier of the cross among ten times ten millions should perish—and for so great a danger as this there is no scientific proof—what then? Is our earthly life so precious that it must be so saved at all hazards? To those who think so, the words of Christ apply: "Whosoever will save his life, shall lose it."

The services provided in Christian churches for the administration of the Lord's Supper by no means neglect its social significance, even if this is not always brought out so fully as some of us might regard as desirable. The chief fault to be found, however, is with the neglect by us at present of what is plainly expressed or clearly implied in our services. Thus the Articles of Religion, both of the Protestant Episcopal and Methodist Episcopal Churches, state: "The Supper of the Lord is not only a sign of the love that Christians ought to have among themselves one to another, but rather is a sacrament of our redemption by Christ's death." The word "rather" lays emphasis upon the Godward side of the Lord's Supper, but this by no means justifies neglect of the social aspects of the sacrament, for these aspects are expressly mentioned and find emphasis in the first position in the article of the words calling attention to them. Furthermore, only those are invited to partake of the Lord's Supper who are "in love and charity with their neighbors." Why? Because love is the essence of the sacrament, and among us men love is fraternity. We approach God in the sacrament of the Lord's Supper as members of the Christian Church; that is to say, of a brotherhood. Malice and hatred violate the sacrament. Do they not crucify afresh the Christ?

Among the sentences which may be read as part of the service is this (and there are many others like it): "Whoso hath this world's goods, and seeth his brother have need, and shutteth up his bowels of compassion from him, how dwelleth the love of God in him?" Most appropriately is the offertory connected with the Lord's Supper.

Our Hymnals, however, seem to be more remote from the full and perfect doctrine of Christ than our Rituals and Prayer Books, for in the Hymnals, under the heading, "The Lord's Supper," there are very few hymns which bring out its social significance—fraternal love.

The import of the Lord's Supper has been well-nigh lost to many Christians. Both its theological significance and social significance have to too many well-nigh disappeared. Early Christians partook of the Lord's Supper daily, but a

Of Baptism and the Lord's Supper. 119

leading divine of a great religious denomination said publicly that he did not attach any peculiar importance to this sacrament. This illustrates the danger of losing sight of the manward aspects of a sacrament of the Church.

May we not well return to primitive Christianity in respect to the Lord's Supper? May it not be possible so to order its observance that it may be more like a common meal, with ceremonies added calculated to emphasize the idea of fraternal love, and celebrate more frequently than most of us do this great sacrament? The author does not venture upon anything more than mere suggestion at this point, and even suggestion he makes with diffidence. Let us, at any rate, restore to the Lord's Supper in our minds and in our hearts and in our practice its full meaning, and may it become more and more precious to us!

We all know the legend of the Holy Grail. It was the cup out of which Jesus drank wine at the last supper with His disciples. It is related that Joseph of Arimathea brought this cup to England, where it long remained an object of adoration, working miracles, restoring health to the diseased, and bringing blessing to those who made pilgrimages to it. It could be kept only by the chaste in thought, word, and deed, and one of the keepers, a lineal descendant of Joseph of Arimathea, failing to preserve this requisite chastity, the cup disappeared.

Tennyson relates the story in these words:

> "The cup, the cup itself, from which our Lord
> Drank at the last sad supper with his own.
> This from the blessed land of Aromat
> After the day of darkness, when the dead
> Went wandering o'er Moriah—the good saint,
> Arimathean Joseph, journeying brought
> To Glastonbury, where the winter thorn
> Blossoms at Christmas, mindful of our Lord,
> And there a while it bode; and if a man
> Could touch or see it, he was healed at once,
> By faith, of all his ills. But then the times
> Grew to such evil that the holy cup
> Was caught away to Heaven, and disappeared."

Knights of the Round Table went in search of the Holy Grail. The quest of Sir Galahad is described by Tennyson in what our own Lowell calls one of his most exquisite poems. But in this poem Tennyson missed the opportunity which Lowell seized in his beautiful poem, "The Vision of Sir Launfal." Sir Launfal, on the eve of going in search of the Holy Grail, has a vision, and in this vision finds the precious treasure. A leper—and in the vision leprosy had once been scorned by Sir Launfal—begs an alms "for Christ's sweet sake." Sir Launfal in his vision had then become "an old, bent man, worn out and frail." His raiment was

Of Baptism and the Lord's Supper. 121

" thin and spare," and himself in want, he replied to the leper:

> " I behold in thee
> An image of Him who died on the tree.
> Thou also hast had thy crown of thorns,—
> Thou also hast had the world's buffets and scorns,—
> And to thy life were not denied,
> The wounds in the hands and feet and side ;
> Mild Mary's Son acknowledge me ;
> Behold, through Him, I give to thee."

Sir Launfal " parted in twain his single crust," shared his all with the beggar. He broke the ice on a stream and dipped out water with a wooden bowl and gave the leper to drink.

> " 'Twas a moldy crust of coarse brown bread,
> 'Twas water out of a wooden bowl,—
> Yet with fine wheaten bread was the leper fed,
> And 'twas red wine he drank with his thirsty soul."

Thus was found the Holy Grail. Sir Launfal partook of the Lord's Supper and through the leper had entered the presence of his Saviour, who addressed him thus:

> " Lo, it is I ; be not afraid!
> In many climes without avail
> Thou hast spent thy life for the Holy Grail ;
> Behold it is here, this cup which thou
> Didst fill at the streamlet for Me, but now;
> This crust is My body broken for thee,
> This water His blood that died on the tree ;
> The Holy Supper is kept, indeed,
> In whatso we share with another's need ;

> Not what we give, but what we share,
> For the gift without the giver is bare;
> Who gives himself with his alms feeds three,
> Himself, his hungering neighbor, and Me."

This is a poet's true interpretation of sacred Scripture. The Holy Grail is within reach of us all. When we worthily, in love with all men, in true sacrificial love, partake of the Lord's Supper, giving ourselves to Christ's flock, we drink from the same cup out of which Jesus partook of the last supper.

Let us not in our optimism, in our hopefulness, be blind to the sin and misery about us, and so miss the opportunity to find the Holy Grail, the cup of love and of sacrifice for us as well as for Christ. Let us not forget that millions of human beings are needlessly sad, needlessly tormented and tortured daily; let us not forget the multitudes who even now in this present life are perishing, are losing their souls; and let us, when we partake of the Lord's Supper, ever pray that we may be strengthened to walk in the footsteps of Christ, loving and serving men as He did; let us resolve to let no day pass without some kind act, something done to make others happier and better. Let us determine, according to the full measure of our resources of body, mind, and estate, to toil without ceasing for the coming of Christ's kingdom. Let us bear constantly in mind the closing acts and words in the life of Him whom we call Lord and Master, namely, the Lord's Supper with His twofold significance, its Godward and manward aspects, the washing of feet, and such commands as these : "If I then, your Lord and Master, have washed your feet; ye also ought to wash one another's feet. For I have given you an example, that ye should do as I have done to you. Verily, verily, I say unto you, The servant is not greater than his Lord; neither he that is sent greater than He that sent him. If ye know these things, happy are ye if ye do them. . . . A new commandment I give unto you, That ye love one another; as I have loved you, that ye also love one another. By this shall all men know that ye are My disciples, if ye have love one to another." [1]

[1] St. John xiii, 14-17, 34, 35.

CHAPTER VI.
SOCIAL SOLIDARITY.

"A SOLITARY individual, in no way connected with fellow-creatures, would have as little opportunity for good as for evil."
—*Baroness von Marenholtz-Bulow, Barnard's Kindergarten and Child Culture, p.* 209.

"What depresses the standard of living in any one class, lowers the level and worth of life throughout the community as a whole."—*Rev. A. M. Fairbairn, D.D., Religion in History and in Modern Life, p.* 8.

"God tells us that He has made man in His own image; not a few particular men who are different from their kind, but the kind itself. And he assuredly who is the most perfect specimen of it, in whom the divine image is fully manifested, will be he who is most entirely at one with the whole race, who the least separates himself even from the most miserable and degraded portions of it."—*F. D. Maurice, Patriarchs and Lawgivers of the Old Testament, p,* 323.

"For I the Lord thy God am a jealous God, visiting the iniquity of the fathers upon the children unto the third and fourth generation of them that hate Me; and showing mercy unto thousands of them that love Me, and keep My commandments."—*Exodus xx,* 5, 6.

CHAPTER VI.

SOCIAL SOLIDARITY.

NOTHING in that associated life of man which we call society is more remarkable than social solidarity. Social solidarity is a principle which underlies a large proportion of all social facts, but one which has received comparatively little attention, and which is probably grasped in its full import by no one. It means so much, and reaches out in so many directions into the social life of men, that it is difficult to give anything like an adequate idea of its true significance. Doubtless we must know more about social solidarity than we do before it will be possible to frame a perfect definition of this principle, which is at the same time a mighty social force. However, there are some things we may say about it.

Social solidarity means the oneness of human interests; it signifies the dependence of man upon man, both in good things and in evil things. Social solidarity means that our true welfare is not an individual matter purely, but likewise a social affair: our weal is common weal;

we thrive only in a commonwealth; our exaltation is the exaltation of our fellows, their elevation is our enlargement. Social solidarity implies not only fellowship in interests and responsibilities, but that unity in nature which is brought before us by the expression, "human brotherhood." Social solidarity signifies not only that man needs association with his fellow-men, but that he shares with them their sins and their sufferings. Our sin is sin for others; their sin is our sin. There is no such thing, either as purely individual sin, or a purely individual righteousness.

Although social philosophy and natural science are just beginning to get a glimmering of the grand truths of social solidarity, the doctrine itself is a very old one. No one has ever given clearer expression to it in its ethical and religious bearings than the Apostle Paul. Human sin comes to us through the human race. The unity of the race is shown in its sin-taint. We are one in our evil character, and in our wrongdoing in which this evil character terminates. This is what is meant in the statement that in Adam we have all sinned. The sin of Adam is not imputed to us in any mechanical fashion, but we have the nature of Adam; that is, the race-nature. "By one man sin entered into the world, and death by sin; and so death passed upon all

Social Solidarity. 129

men, in that all have sinned."[1] "In Adam all die."[2] This states the law of social solidarity on its passive side; but it is stated with equal plainness in its active aspects: "For as by one man's disobedience many were made sinners, so by the obedience of one shall many be made righteous."[3] "For as in Adam all die, even so in Christ shall all be made alive."[4]

The doctrine of social solidarity is brought forward again and again throughout the entire Bible, from Genesis to Revelation, and is, indeed, one of the most remarkable features of this wonderful book. It is clearly expressed in that part of the Bible which deals with the human race before the time of Abraham; and the entire history of the Jews, both in their internal relations and their relations to foreign nations, emphasizes social solidarity. The nation rejoices together and suffers together; the nation partakes of the benefits of the righteousness of the righteous, and is punished on account of the wrongdoings of the wicked. The active power of a few righteous men is told us in the history of Abraham's pleading for Sodom, the city of Lot. The Lord promised that should but ten righteous men be found in the city it would not be destroyed for the ten's sake. But when Israel

[1] Romans v, 12. [2] 1 Corinthians xv, 22.
[3] Romans v, 19. [4] 1 Corinthians xv, 22.

departs from God and no longer maintains righteous relations among men, and when the rich oppress the poor and the strong make a prey of the feeble, then the nation is led away into captivity. And this is all easily enough understood. It is the legitimate outcome of natural laws established by God. And these laws are still operative, and their working in the history of Israel is written for our admonition.

When we come to the New Testament we have taught, with even greater force, the law of social solidarity. But there is that difference which has been pointed out in general between the Old and the New Testaments. The law is not merely national but universal, and it becomes more intensive. If we collectively, as well as individually, seek the kingdom of God, all material blessings will be added unto us. Let it not be forgotten that it is the kingdom which we are to seek, and a kingdom is a social state. Many a theologian interprets the passage as if it read, individual salvation, and not the kingdom of God. The few may prosper materially through unrighteous social relations, but it is only through right social relations that the many can thrive. "Righteousness exalteth a nation." So long as wrong relations exist among men, the righteous man, the man who seeks the kingdom of God, may suffer in material things on account of his righteousness. A mistake is often made by a too narrow interpretation of Christ's words. When we forget that Christ spoke of the coming of His kingdom continually, and always had this kingdom in His mind, we are apt to interpret individually what He intended should be taken as applicable to society. When a condition of things exists like that found in Jerusalem in Christ's time, a man may seek the kingdom of God, and yet may be persecuted even unto death. In the Epistle to the Hebrews we read of the prophets who subdued kingdoms and did many wonderful works, and of whom the world was not worthy; that they were stoned and sawn asunder; that "they wandered about in sheepskins and goatskins; being destitute, afflicted, and tormented."[1]

This oneness of men was peculiarly close among the followers of Christ, for they are spoken of again and again as "one body." "We are one body in Christ, and everyone members one of another."[2] In another place it is said we are members of Christ's body, "of His flesh and of His bones."[3] Christ ardently longed for a more perfect union with His disciples than that which existed, and He prayed for His disciples that remarkable prayer recorded in the seventeenth chapter of the Gospel According to

[1] Hebrews, chapter xi.   [2] Romans xii, 5.   [3] Ephesians v, 30.

St. John, containing these words: "Neither pray I for these alone, but for them also which shall believe on Me through their word; that they all may be one; as Thou, Father, art in Me, and I in Thee, that they also may be one in Us: that the world may believe that Thou hast sent Me. And the glory which Thou gavest Me I have given them; that they may be one, even as We are one."

If we read the words of Christ in the light of this doctrine of social solidarity, we shall find in them a meaning which probably has escaped most of us. This doctrine does not take away anything from what we have rightly held dear, but it adds new fullness and depth to Christ's teachings. We find Christ again and again rebuking those who would separate themselves from their fellows, who thought they could exalt themselves above their fellows, and believed that they were free from the wrongs which prevailed all about them. Again and again Christ convicts those self-righteous people of their iniquities. One of the most remarkable instances is given in the narrative of the woman taken in the very act of sin. She was brought to Christ, and He was reminded of the law of Moses that such a woman should suffer death. He was asked what should be done with her. Christ commanded that he who was without sin should cast the first stone, and "they which heard it went out one by one, beginning at the eldest, even unto the last."[1] This by no means signifies that each one of those Pharisees had been guilty of this very act, but that they all shared in the common guilt, for they had not done what might have been done to banish sin and to restore men to righteousness. They neglected sinners and did not seek to save the lost.

Social solidarity relieves the weak and erring, it is very true, of a part of their individual guilt; and for this reason doubtless Christ was so gentle with this class, but on the whole it increases individual responsibility immensely. This is unconsciously admitted in the very general desire to escape social responsibility. We are responsible to a certain extent for all the poverty and sin and suffering about us. An entire city is guilty on account of the murder which occurs in some alley in a slum; yet whoever utters a word publicly which tends to separate men out from the common lot of their fellows, and to assist them in an evasion of their share of social responsibility, is a speaker sure of a warm welcome, and what he says will pass readily from newspaper to newspaper throughout the entire length and breadth of the land.

Writers of deep insight have given frequent

[1] St. John viii, 9.

expression to the great truths of social solidarity. Hawthorne says: " While there is a single guilty person in the universe, each innocent one must feel his innocence tortured by that guilt." Margaret Fuller utters a similar thought in these words: "While one man remains base, no man can be altogether great and noble." Matthew Arnold expresses the principle of social solidarity in these words: "Culture, or the study of perfection, leads us to conceive of no perfection as being real which is not a general perfection, embracing all our fellow-men with whom we have to do. Such is the sympathy which binds humanity together that we are, indeed, as our religion says, ' members of one body,' and if 'one member suffer, all the members suffer with it.' Individual perfection is impossible so long as the rest of mankind are not perfected along with us."

Man is the son of man, the blood of the race flows in his veins. If we trace back our ancestry we find that the lines of our descent cross and recross almost to infinity. Thus it is a true saying that " society gives us ancestors." Recent interest in families awakened by organizations, like the " Daughters of the Revolution," shows how all the old New England families and all the old Virginia families are related, and closer research gives an immense network embracing both sections. The lines in reality extend much farther than anyone thinks, because in certain directions these lines are not pleasing and consequently not followed out. We lose the threads which would enable us to trace back our ancestry very soon, but we can go far enough to furnish at least strong evidences of a unity of considerable proportion of the race, and science can carry the proof much farther. There is a race-blood given as our inheritance, carrying with it tendencies and capacities. Man is born into a moral atmosphere; he breathes it in and shares in its guilt and in its excellence. At first the moral quality is given, and the early development of personality takes place on the basis of what is given. Responsibility of the individual increases with age. The individual is first a result, but later becomes a cause. Early individual irresponsibility is recognized by the courts of all civilized lands, equally with growing responsibility.

Investigations into causes of physical infirmities, like deafness and blindness, show very generally wrongdoing on the part of some ancestor. Quite frequently this wrongdoing takes the form indicated by alcoholism. The child suffers for sins committed before his birth.[1] Investigations

[1] When the author not long since listened to a series of lectures on the defective and unfortunate classes, he was impressed with the frequency with which this thought was advanced by the various experts who delivered the lectures.

into causes of crime and pauperism show us a network of evil forces indicated by the two words, "heredity" and "environment," surrounding thousands and hundreds of thousands at their very birth. Those more fortunate ones, well-born physically, mentally, and morally, are apt to turn away in scorn from the unfortunate and degenerate classes, and to neglect the opportunities which are abundant to improve the conditions under which they live. It was to such as these that Christ gave warning that those upon whom the tower in Siloam fell were not guilty above all the other dwellers at Jerusalem, but that unless they repented they should likewise perish. So it is with us; wretchedness and disease travel from class to class and from individual to individual.

We may trace social solidarity into every department of our common life. If we take it on its physiological side, we find that physically we suffer together: "The whole creation groaneth and travaileth in pain together until now."[1] This was understood in a general way long ago, but in the modern study of disease it has received scientific demonstration. The whole world is bound together in the chains of disease. Mohammedans gather together in multitudes in a city in Persia at a time of unusual drought, and

[1] Romans viii, 22.

cholera begins to make its way round the world. There is a crop failure in five provinces of Russia, and during the ensuing famine Russian peasants die by the thousand. In this suffering region we find the origin of the grippe which has carried away hundreds of thousands in Europe and the United States. Still more closely are all parts of one country, and more especially of one city, connected together in health and disease. Says Dr. Cyrus Edson in a remarkable article on the subject: "While the communities have, through their Boards of Health, prepared for the battle with contagious diseases, and while they can trust with perfect confidence to their defenses, the work of the men employed in these Boards reveals to them more clearly day by day the close connection which exists between the health interests of all members of the community, be these rich or poor; the microbe of disease is no respecter of persons; it cannot be guarded against by any bank account, however large."[1] Nevertheless, it is true that a bank account is a help, although no sure guarantee. Persons of wealth live much longer than the poor, but in so far as they escape the common consequences of disease their moral responsibility increases, and morally they are the more

[1] See " The Microbe as a Social Leveler," *North American Review*, October, 1895.

guilty if they do not use their larger resources to establish conditions of health for all.

Social solidarity may also be traced in things intellectual. Our intellectual products are peculiarly individual, and yet they are all dependent upon conditions which no one man has established or could establish. A Shakespeare could not arise in the heart of Africa, nor could we find a Tennyson to-day in China. Man has achieved his greatest and best in intellectual efforts of every sort when surrounded by a large life. When man speaks nobly the race speaks through him and he speaks for the race. Witness the great eras of literature and art in Greece, in Rome, in England.

Political solidarity is something so old and so familiar that we need scarcely more than mention it. We are all responsible for the political acts of our country, both with our persons and with our property. If those who manage the affairs of the nation act foolishly we may lose both our goods and our lives. Punishment for the sins of the rulers is a fact as old as history, yet the rulers of nations do not stand alone. As John Wesley says, "God frequently punishes a people for the sins of their rulers, because they are generally partakers of their sins in one kind or other."[1]

It is a peculiar fact that social solidarity grows

---

[1] John Wesley's sermon, "National Sins and Miseries," in his *Sermons*, vol. I, p. 515.

with the growth of civilization; men come closer and closer together and the unity of the race becomes more and more intensive. This is best of all illustrated in that department of life in which it is most marked; namely, economics. To a greater and greater extent we are dependent on others for the conditions of our own prosperity. It has been pointed out in modern society that man is dependent for his economic well-being, first, upon what he himself produces; second, upon the exertions of others who produce the things which he wants in exchange for his own products; third, upon the efforts of others who produce the same things which he produces, giving us competition among sellers; fourth, upon the efforts of those who want the things that he wants, giving us competition among purchasers. Along one line, then, man is dependent upon himself; along three lines, he is dependent upon the efforts of others. The man who produces only shoes would starve to death did not others work for him, while he works for them. As the division of labor is carried farther and farther, economic dependence increases, and thus social solidarity grows.

The author has a friend connected with a hospital whose experience shows what an awful thing it is for a man to get out of human relations, either because he has sundered the essential ties of humanity, or because they have been sundered for him by others, or because, for him, perchance, they have never existed. The waifs, the strays, the morally abandoned, frequently have no special tie binding them to anyone. This friend of the author makes inquiry into the personal relations of those coming to the hospital; he asks especially, in case of possible death, "Who cares for you, what relative have you?" and like questions. Frequently the reply is, "No one." To upbuild human character in men you must establish for them right social relations. On the other hand, we fulfill our own mission and develop our own true individuality, not in isolation, but in society, and by bringing ourselves in body and mind into harmony with the laws of social solidarity.

CHAPTER VII.
OUR NEIGHBORS.

"A CERTAIN lawyer . . . said unto Jesus, And who is my neighbor? And Jesus answering said, A certain man went down from Jerusalem to Jericho, and fell among thieves, which stripped him of his raiment, and wounded him, and departed, leaving him half dead. And by chance there came down a certain priest that way; and when he saw him, he passed by on the other side. And likewise a Levite, when he was at the place, came and looked on him, and passed by on the other side. But a certain Samaritan, as he journeyed, came where he was ; and when he saw him, he had compassion on him, and went to him, and bound up his wounds, pouring in oil and wine, and set him on his own beast, and brought him to an inn, and took care of him. And on the morrow when he departed, he took out two pence, and gave them to the host, and said unto him, Take care of him : and whatsoever thou spendest more, when I come again, I will repay thee. Which now of these three, thinkest thou, was neighbor unto him that fell among the thieves? And he said, He that showed mercy on him. Then said Jesus unto him, Go, and do thou likewise."—*St. Luke x*, 25–37.

"The intent of the similitude is to show to whom a man is a neighbor, or who is a man's neighbor, which is both one, and what it is to love a man's neighbor as himself. The Samaritan holp him, and showed mercy as long as he was present ; and when he could be no longer present, he left his money behind him, and if that were not sufficient, he left his credence to make good the rest ; and forsook him not, as long as the other had need. Then said Christ, ' Go, thou, and do likewise ; ' that is, without difference or respection of persons ; whosoever needeth thy help, him count thy neighbor, and his neighbor be thou, and show mercy on him as long as he needeth thy succor, and that is to love a man's neighbor as himself. Neighbor is a word of love ; and signifieth that a man should be ever nigh, and at hand, and ready to help in time of need."—*Tyndale, The Wicked Mammon, Parker Society Publications, p.* 85.

CHAPTER VII.

OUR NEIGHBORS.

A QUOTATION from Sir Henry Maine will serve as a text for the present chapter. It reads as follows:

"What is the real origin of the feeling that it is not creditable to drive a hard bargain with a near relative or friend? It can hardly be said that there is any rule of morality to forbid it. The feeling seems to me to bear the traces of the old notion that men united in natural groups do not deal with one another on principles of trade. . . . The general proposition which is the basis of political economy made its first approach to truth under the only circumstances which admitted of men meeting at arm's length, not as brothers of the same group, but as strangers. . . . If the notion of getting the best price for movable property has only crept to reception by insensible steps, it is all but certain that the idea of taking the highest obtainable rent for land is relatively of very modern origin. The rent of land corresponds to the price of goods, but doubtless was infinitely slower in conforming to economical law, since the impression of a brotherhood in the ownership of land still survived when goods had long since become the subject of individual property."

The ancient village community was an association of men bound together by peculiarly close ties. These men were generally supposed to be descended from a common ancestor and thus to be more or less closely related, and any outsiders received into the community became members of this large family. They felt themselves to be brothers, and in an imperfect manner attempted to establish brotherly relations among themselves. Competition was greatly restrained—in fact, in the modern sense could hardly be said to exist—custom regulated prices, and sharp practice and hard bargaining were viewed with disapprobation and often severely punished. Ethical obligation extended to all the relations of life. The range of this obligation, however, was not extensive; once outside the community, moral law was scarcely recognized. There was often a place touching three or four village communities, but not belonging to any one, which was neutral territory. This became a market where the customs and usages of the village community no longer held sway, and it was in this market that the idea of the legitimacy of hard bargaining and sharp practice took its origin, as we are told by

Sir Henry Maine. This authority regards sharp practice and hard bargaining as true economic practice, and inquires why it is that somehow or other men are still frequently inclined to view it with disapprobation. He finds the explanation in survivals of feelings which once obtained among closely connected groups of men. The highest rent obtainable for land is not always exacted in England, and it is said that there are places where such an exaction would ostracise the land-owner. The explanation given is that manorial groups were substituted for village communities, and that they still survive, even if in imperfect form.

As old groups of men broke up with modern progress, ethical ideas have seemed to become weaker, and there has been an attempt to take one great department of social life, namely, the economic, entirely outside the range of ethical obligation. Ancient groups were associations of brothers, but those not within the groups were enemies. The three words, foreigner, stranger, and enemy, were similar, and often the same word denoted all three relationships—that of foreigner, that of stranger, and that of enemy. When men's dealings were chiefly with those not connected by any recognized tie of mutual obligation, each one naturally tried to do the best he could for himself, regardless of consequences to others. Yet there never has been a time when there have not been those associations of one sort and another within which ordinarily good men have viewed with disapprobation hard bargaining. It may be said, indeed, that a genuine feeling of brotherhood is incompatible with sharp practice and hard bargaining, and Sir Henry Maine is altogether on the wrong track when he looks for a time when what he styles economic practices shall universally obtain, and men shall applaud that person who drives a hard bargain or indulges in sharp practice with neighbors and friends. The breakdown of old ties which were intensive and not extensive led to a great weakening in the intensity of ethical feeling, especially in business life, because the same amount of feeling was, if such an expression may be used, made to cover a territory so much larger. Men, however, have long been taught in all civilized nations that all men are brothers, and most enlightened persons profess to accept this teaching of universal brotherhood. There has been, then, an extension of brotherhood which is simply immense, placing us in the modern world indefinitely in advance of the closely related but exclusive groups of the ancient world. The range of ethical obligation has been widened until it embraces all humanity, but it has not been deepened in proportion.

Our Neighbors. 147

The work of deepening this feeling, however, goes on uninterruptedly.

Day by day the phrase, "All men are brothers," comes to mean more and more, and the time is surely coming when it will ethically mean as much in the world at large as once it did in the village community; and when that time comes no decent man will any longer advocate the legitimacy of the universal sway of sharp practice and hard bargaining. Men will then try to put all business relations upon a brotherly basis, and will always inquire what forms of industrial organization and what modes of doing business are in accordance with the highest standards of right, and best promote the general welfare. It is this deepening process of ethical obligation which explains many social problems of our day. The deepening is going on with remarkable rapidity, and the result is that men everywhere are bringing to bear ethical tests upon all relations of life, and are rejecting as unsound all practices and customs inconsistent with genuine brotherhood. Mere conventional phrases no longer satisfy us; we want the reality of brotherhood. Now, a business world which has taken its origin in middle ground lying between communities within which the range of ethical obligation was confined can never satisfy a highly developed Christian consciousness. Men may talk and argue as they will about economic law, yet there is deep down in our hearts a feeling that there is something better than sharp practice and hard bargaining.

It was an unbelieving age of materialism which asserted the all-sufficiency and even beneficence of unrestrained self-interest, and attempted to restrict economic inquiries to this one question: "How produce the greatest amount of wealth?" Aristotle, Plato, and the wisest of the ancients never asked, "How can our nation become as rich as possible?" but rather, "How may such economic and social relations be established among citizens as to render them good and happy?" They sought in the business world merely a basis for the highest physical, mental, and spiritual development of man, but they never looked upon the accumulation of riches as an end in itself. These ancients did not extend the range of ethical obligation beyond nationality, but our age regards all men as closely connected as the Jews in the eyes of Moses or the Greeks in the mind of Plato. Consequently we begin to ask similar questions.

The widening and deepening range of ethical obligation rests upon a basis of solid facts. One of the most characteristic features of the latter half of the nineteenth century is the extension of international connections. Men of all nations are drawing nearer and nearer together in every department of social life. After men ceased to regard the foreigner as necessarily an enemy, they long continued to consider him as an inferior. Doubtless there are still Americans who regard Americans as superior to Englishmen or Germans or Frenchmen; but as knowledge extends and practical Christianity advances we feel that God has created all men of one blood. This is seen in international marriages, which have their good side, and that one of no mean significance. The number daily increases of those who have ties of blood relationship extending to several countries. It often happens that people of culture and means have friends in three or four countries, and dear friends with whom connection is kept up by correspondence and occasional interchange of visits.

The freedom with which capital moves from country to country has become a matter of common knowledge, and it is often said that capital knows no country, but is strictly cosmopolitan. This is, to be sure, an exaggeration, but it emphasizes forcibly actual facts. The past generation has witnessed a marvelous growth of a feeling of brotherhood among the wage-earners of modern industrial nations. Possibly when the history of the nineteenth century comes to be written, several generations hence, this will be regarded as the most marvelous feature of the second half of the century. The ties which bind workingmen to workingmen all over the world are very real, and are felt wherever there is an intelligent wage-earning class with a developed class-consciousness. Papers devoted to the interests of labor published in every European country find their way to the United States, and our labor papers find their way to all European countries. Even Asia and Africa are coming into this world movement. Workingmen of one nation contribute to those of others to assist them in their upward struggle, and refuse advantages procured at the expense of brothers whom they have never seen. Why cite facts when all know that contributions of Australian workingmen helped English workingmen to a victory in one of the most momentous struggles with their employers, and when the fact has frequently been published that workingmen from the Continent of Europe who have been brought to England to take the place of strikers have returned to their own countries as soon as they found out the true nature of their engagement, and when under similar circumstances European workingmen have even crossed the ocean from America to Europe after they had come over here in the hope of finding better wages?

The extension of the range of ethical obligation moves most readily along what may be called horizontal lines—that is to say, it is largely an extension within social classes. The English merchant recognizes ties which bind him to the merchant in New York and Paris and Berlin. Manufacturers and employers generally are more and more conscious of relations of brotherhood binding them together, and as has just been stated, the wage-earners of all lands feel their oneness, and their great rallying cry has gone forth: " Workingmen of all lands, unite!" Thus it often happens that there is a better understanding among members of any one industrial class in different countries than among members of different industrial classes in the same country. It cannot, indeed, be denied that while industrial and social classes in different countries are drawing together, there is in some places a growing hostility often separating class from class in the same country; yet there is also in many quarters evidence of efforts to bring together into brotherly relations all classes. The range of ethical obligation is in this respect likewise deepening. We are more and more inclined to put ourselves in the place of those who socially or industrially are differently situated from ourselves, and hence it is that so many young men and women of means and culture are devoting themselves in social settlements, like Hull House in Chicago, and elsewhere, to social problems in the hope of ameliorating the condition of the less favored portions of humanity, and that in great centers of education, like Oxford, we find an admirable enthusiasm of humanity which, in its earnestness and intensity, can only be compared with the crusades.

Those of us who belong to what would ordinarily be called the cultured, well-to-do, and influential classes in the community, ought to make it clear to ourselves that we are still very far from ethical fairness in our dealings with the less favored social classes and in the judgments which we pass upon them. We have one measure which we apply to the acts and utterances of those in our own social class, and another measure which we apply to the acts and utterances of those belonging to other social classes, in particular the wage-earning classes. Let a dispute arise between employers and employed, and we at once accept the statement of the employers. This is given to the press, and this alone as a rule; yet we pass judgment without trying to find out what the workingmen could say for themselves. If, however, two employers quarrel, we suspend judgment until we have heard both sides. We assume, moreover, that the obligations which rest upon workingmen are different and far severer than those which apply to their employers. Journals of the highest respectability will assure us that employers have a perfect right to refuse to treat with a representative of the employees, whereas they would regard it as a most unwarrantable impertinence and impudence if workingmen should refuse to deal with any one whom their employers might select as a delegate. The writer has in mind a strike which occurred some two years ago, and a prominent newspaper in New York said that the employers had an undoubted right to refuse to treat with outsiders assuming to represent the wage-earners. There is no doubt, however, on the part of any honest and well-informed man that these representatives were genuine representatives. Let us reverse the case and suppose the strikers—who in this case happened to be street-car employees —should refuse to treat with some delegate of the capitalists, claiming that he was an outsider, owning no part of the capital invested in the street railway.

Another incident which occurred during this same strike shows how unequal and unfair are our judgments. What is called an iron-clad agreement was presented to the workingmen, forcing them to withdraw from all labor organizations as a condition of employment. This was regarded by many papers—and among them even religious papers—as perfectly fair and proper. Let us reverse the case. Employers have their associations, and one of the avowed designs of these associations is the regulation and control of labor. To deny this is simply a confession of ignorance or dishonesty. Suppose these workingmen had united and presented an "iron-clad" to their employers, refusing to work for them unless they dissolved connection with all associations of employers. Would not editorials innumerable have been penned and sermons many been preached in denunciation of these workingmen? Employers have a right to conduct their own business as they please within limits, but this does not involve their one-sided regulation of conditions under which employees must work and the selection of associates with whom they must work. When workingmen interfere in business—as it is claimed by their employers—it is usually to regulate those conditions which are of importance to themselves. Very rarely do workingmen attempt to interfere with employers in the conduct of their business except in so far as it is a matter of direct and immediate concern to themselves. What must be said about such controversies as this from the standard of ethical fairness?

We may ask this question: Is there a growing feeling of ethical obligation on the part of the wage-earning classes with respect to their employers? Do they feel more and more that they must give good work for good pay? Do they feel, to an increasing extent, that their work is an ethical calling; that they have a mission in God's world to minister to the happiness and well-being of society? Do they always greet with warm appreciation self-sacrificing efforts made in their behalf? Unfortunately, while recognizing the high and conscientious and truly Christian conduct of many wage-earners, a negative answer must be returned. If we speak of the richer and employing classes as higher and the poorer and wage-earning classes as lower social classes—and to refuse to do so is to refuse to acknowledge facts as they exist—we must say that the downward movement in the extension of the range of ethical obligation has in recent years been stronger than the upward one. The favored classes are to some extent trying to atone for the shortcomings of past centuries. This is well; but it is also right that earnest endeavors should be made in all kindness to quicken the consciences of wage-earners especially, and generally the less favored social classes, to a realizing sense of their duties and obligations, for, like all others, working people have been thinking too much about rights and too little about duties. Even a feeling on the part of wage-earners, that the present social order is one which ought to be changed, cannot be held to free them from obligations to their employers and to others.

In conclusion, while in view of what remains to be accomplished we can scarcely say that we have made more than a beginning, we may nevertheless characterize our age as one in which may be perceived a clearly defined widening and deepening range of ethical obligation.

CHAPTER VIII.
THE STATE.

"Our patriotic duty is our Christian duty."—*Rev. E. A. Schell, D.D., Secretary of the Epworth League, in an address entitled "Methodism, a Layman's Movement."*

"From history we learn that the great function of religion has been the founding and sustaining of States."—*Sir J. R. Seeley, Natural Religion, p. 202.*

"The State—the greatest institution on earth—elevates everything that appertains to it, every duty, interest, or measure, into great importance, for the simple reason that it affects all, and, what with its direct and indirect operation, it very materially influences the moral well-being of every individual. . . . Good laws elevate man ; bad laws, if persisted in for a series of years, will degrade any society. . . . It is one of the greatest blessings to live under wise laws administered by an upright government, and obeyed and carried out by good and stanch citizens; it is most grateful and animating to a generous heart, and a mind which cheerfully assists in the promotion of the general good, or salutary institutions. It greatly contributes to our self-esteem if we live in a community which we respect, among fellow-men we gladly acknowledge as fellow-citizens. Many of the noblest actions which now adorn the pages of history have originated from this source of inspiration. On the contrary, we feel ourselves humbled and dispirited, we find our own views contracted and our moral vigor relaxed, we feel deprived of that buoyancy without which no manly and resolute self-possession can exist, it wears off the edge of moral sensitiveness when we see ourselves surrounded by men with loose political principles, by a society destitute of active public opinion, which neither cheers the honest nor frowns down immoral boldness."—*Francis Lieber, LL.D., Political Ethics, Edited by Theodore D. Woolsey, pp. 79, 80.*

"In order then to the chief good, the righteous man must live in a righteous state ; virtue within and virtue without must dwell together in beautiful and holy unity. But if God means that each person realize the chief good, what ideal does He set before us for society? This: That the individuals composing it shall, every one of them, be perfectly virtuous, or perfectly holy, and that the State into which they are organized shall in every respect be perfectly ordered and perfectly righteous, an altogether good and holy State. No less an ideal as respects man, on the one hand, and society, on the other, can satisfy the Christian idea of God."—*Rev. A. M. Fairbairn, D.D., Religion in History and in Modern Life, p.* 257.

"We wait for the next stage in the growth of the State, when in full and generous cooperation each citizen shall offer the fullness of his own life, that he may rejoice in the fullness of the life of the body. Such an issue may appear to be visionary. It is, I believe, far nearer than we suppose. It is at least the natural outcome of what has gone before. Society has been organized effectively without regard to the individual. The individual has been developed in his independence. It remains to show how the richest variety of individual differences can be made to fulfillt he noblest ideal of the State."—*From an address by Bishop B. F. Westcott at the Church, reprinted in " Christian Socialism" by Rev. Philo W. Sprague.*

CHAPTER VIII.

THE STATE.

THE word State is, in the United States especially, liable to be misunderstood, when it is used in its generic sense. Our United States is made up of forty-five commonwealths, and these are called states. But State in its most general sense is not equivalent to state in the sense of the American commonwealth. The State means the entire American nation, politically organized. The American State embraces the American in all his political relations, as the German State embraces the German in all his political relations. The English State and the French State similarly embrace the Englishmen and Frenchmen respectively in all their political relations. The Americans, however, like the Germans, have a federal State, while the English and the French have a unitary State. We might therefore, in the present chapter, when speaking of Americans, substitute for State "the nation and the commonwealth," because both make up our State, but the substitution would be objectionable, first, because it would involve the use of three words where one is sufficient, and this would frequently be awkward; second, because it is desirable that we should become accustomed to the use of the word State in its generic sense and remember our relations to nation and commonwealth alike.

Commonwealth is often used as equivalent of State as later in this chapter. If a commonwealth has full and complete sovereignty, it is of course a State in its complete sense. In the United States, the nation and commonwealth must be taken together to give complete sovereignty. The word State is used in this broad sense both in John Wesley's "Sunday Service" and in the revised book of Common Prayer of the Protestant Episcopal Church in the petition, "O Lord, save the State."

Family, Church, and State are frequently mentioned together as the three pre-eminently divine institutions known to man. It is claimed by some that the State is the chief institution of these three, and that if we select one institution as above all others divine it must be the State. Such a comparison manifestly cannot be understood too literally. If several institutions are established by God, it can hardly be strictly true that one is more divine than another. What is meant is this: That God works through the State in carrying out His purposes more universally

The State. 163

than through any other institution ; that it takes the first place among His instrumentalities.

The family is clearly a divine institution. The Bible leaves no doubt about this in the mind of anyone who accepts the Bible as true. Destroy the family and you destroy one of the fundamental conditions of that righteousness which God desires to establish. Yet the family is not inclusive of all men, like the State. Most men are undoubtedly born into this world as members of a family, and not to be included in a family at one's birth is abnormal and most unfortunate. Yet as men grow up they must leave the family, if, as not infrequently happens, death has not already destroyed it. Many of those scattered elements of former families unite and form new families ; yet there are always large numbers living isolated lives, forming no part of any family. Not only has this always been the case, but it always must be ; and there is some reason to believe that it will be the case to even a greater extent in the future than at present. There are physical reasons why many men and women should not marry and establish families, and there are economic reasons. Men otherwise amiable and intelligent occasionally lack the capacity to support a family according to the standard of life suitable to their station. Physical and economic reasons for a single life will be more appreciated, as men become more conscientious about assuming responsibilities toward others. Disparity between the number of men and the number of women in most parts of the earth is a cause of singleness. It is not to the point to reply that the whole number of men in the world is nearly equal to the number of women, provided they are not evenly distributed. A bachelor in Montana cannot marry a spinster in Germany. The more dangerous avocations of men tend to reduce the supply of available husbands. Again there are humanitarian and religious motives which keep men and women from marrying. Christ ranked such motives very high, and promises great rewards to those who for His sake give up husband or wife. Much more might be said about the family and its limitations, but space will not admit of it. The State includes now and always has included within its embrace all civilized men and women, but only some of these, and not all, belong to distinct families or households.

The Church, as we understand it, began to exist less than two thousand years ago; but long before the apostles of Christ established the Church God worked in the world, and the institution through which He worked above all others was the State. His chosen people, the Jews, constituted a commonwealth established, we are told, by God. The revelation of God to the Jews, and through the Jews to the rest of the world, is found in the laws and in the life of the Hebrew State. These laws and this life were an inspiration to David and the other poets of Israel, and they were the prime object of solicitude to the prophets. The prophets, in fact, were statesmen, or, if you will, politicians, in the nobler sense of the word. When Christ came His mind was full of the kingdom or commonwealth in which righteousness should prevail. The coming of the kingdom was proclaimed by Christ, and it was His followers who began to talk about a Church as distinct from the State. The Church was early established, and it has increased in numbers and in power, but it has never embraced more than a minority of civilized human beings. There have always been followers of God who have not been adherents of any visible Church, any regularly established ecclesiastical organization, but these are all embraced within the State, and the State also includes those outside sinners, those unregenerate persons who do not love God and man, and do not seek righteousness, among whom the Church works.

We must ever remember that Christ and His apostles always recognized the authority of the State as divine in character even under most trying and perplexing circumstances. Christ counscled obedience to the Roman emperor, and St. Paul uses well-known words which could scarcely be more explicit: " For there is no power but of God : the powers that be are ordained of God.

" Whosoever therefore resisteth the power, resisteth the ordinance of God. . . .

" For rulers are not a terror to good works, but to the evil. Wilt thou then not be afraid of the power? do that which is good, and thou shalt have praise of the same:

" For he is the minister of God to thee for good. But if thou do that which is evil, be afraid ; for he beareth not the sword in vain: for he is the minister of God. . . .

" For this cause pay ye tribute also. . . .

" Render therefore to all their dues : tribute to whom tribute is due ; custom to whom custom; fear to whom fear ; honor to whom honor."[1]

It has also been pointed out that while Christ manifested no respect for mere wealth or assumed titles, he never failed to show obedience and honor to the regularly constituted public authorities.[2]

So essential is the State to the work of God in this world, that if missionaries penetrate into a

---

[1] Romans xiii, 1–7.
[2] By Rev. F. W. Robertson in his sermon, " The Message of the Church to Men of Wealth," in the volume of his *Sermons*.

The State. 167

stateless region, say, the heart of Africa, and convert men to Christianity, those men will at once form a new State, or become incorporated as part of an old State. All great and glorious deeds of men have taken place within a State, and the highest achievements of the mind of man have been preceded or accompanied by a large and expanding national life.

The State has been described as a continuous, conscious organism, and a moral personality, which has its foundations laid in the nature of man. It is not the product of the will of man. Men have never come together in a state of nature, and then by the formation of a State passed out of a condition of nature into an organized political existence. The State grows up naturally, spontaneously, and men are born into the State, and the State is one of the forces making them what they are. The basis of the State is human nature, and the State is the natural condition of men. Some would have us to go to savages to find out what is natural, but Aristotle has taught us that it is the perfect man, and not the imperfect man, who can reveal to us what is natural, just as we look at a perfect and not an imperfect specimen of fruit to understand the nature of the fruit.

Aristotle described an order of development when he said the State was formed for the sake of life, but that it was continued for the sake of the good life. This means that the State is necessary in order that man may live at all. Its first purpose was the provision of material resources for the nourishment of the animal life, but the higher, nobler purpose of the State is not the material life, but the soul and mind of man. As soon as the means of life are provided, we must aspire to the good life. The ignoble doctrine that the State is a necessary evil was as far from Aristotle as it has been from all great political thinkers. The State was to him not only a necessary good, but the highest and noblest of all good.

For a long time previous to the Protestant Reformation false notions concerning the Church obscured the idea of the State. It was held by leaders in the Church that the Church was noble because it was concerned with spiritual things, and that the State was base because it was concerned with temporal things. Consequently it was maintained that the Church should dominate the State, as the spirit ought to rule the body. The rulers of the State were to be the servants of priests, humbly doing their bidding. The Protestant Reformation meant the exaltation of the State. The truth was proclaimed with emphasis that the work which God intended His people to do while on earth was to concern themselves with the things of the world, and to establish here on earth righteous relations among men. The wide separation between things secular and things sacred was denied. The whole earth was held sacred. Nothing was secular in any bad sense of the word except sin, and the purpose of Christians was to combat it. As soon as it was recognized that the work given to Christians was the establishment of righteousness, the function of the magistrate became as sacred as that of the priest. One of the reformers uses these words, expressing a belief of early Protestantism: " The distinction of ecclesiastical and profane laws can find no place among Christians. The magistrate himself is holy and not profane, his powers and laws holy, his sword holy." This exalted idea of the State was followed by most momentous practical consequences. The State began to concern itself with education, and schools and universities became State institutions, and the educational work of the State continued until in the most enlightened Protestant nations every child was guaranteed at least a minimum amount of education. The cry of the poor became a matter of concern to the civil authorities, and in Protestant Teutonic countries the right of man to at least a bare livelihood was guaranteed by the Poor Laws. The obligation to maintain the poor was for the first time assumed by civil society in the sixteenth century, after the Protestant Reformation. Another consequence of the exaltation of the State was the curtailment of the functions of ecclesiastical Courts and the extension of the function of the civil Courts, to which all alike, clergy included, ultimately became subject. If the civil sword was holy and civil justice divine, why should there exist a separate ecclesiastical jurisdiction arrogating superiority to itself?[1]

The only limit to the functions of the State is that laid down by Aristotle; the general principle cannot be stated better than he stated it: "It is the duty of the State to do whatever is in its power to promote the good life." Any other limitation is false to the fundamental principles of Protestantism, both ancient and modern. The venerable Hooker repudiated with these vigorous words the doctrine that the State existed only for the sake of material goods: "A gross error it is to think that regal power ought to serve for the good of the body, and not for the good of the soul; for men's temporal peace, and not their eternal safety; and if God had

[1] The author does not understand that there is anything in this paragraph which a Roman Catholic must of necessity reject. Every enlightened Roman Catholic acknowledges that those claiming to speak and act for the Church have made many mistakes. The writer, however, speaks from the Protestant point of view, but can only rejoice if Roman Catholics also can accept what is here stated, as he is convinced many of them can.

ordained kings for no other end and purpose but only to fat up men like hogs and see that they have their mast?"[1]

The imperfect political life of our time, especially in our own country, may be thought by some to be antagonistic to the doctrine of the divinity of the State. The divinity of an institution, however, does not mean its perfection in its actual existence, but only in its idea. God has given us the idea, and we have carried it out poorly. The State is, alas, corrupt and degraded; but so have been also the Church and the family at many times and in many places. The polygamy of the Mormons no more militates against the divine idea of the family than the corruption of New York politics against the divine idea of the State. Government is divine in idea and purpose, but those in New York city who administer government are too generally unworthy of their high trust. One reason why political life in the United States is so unworthy is because the true idea of the State has become so obscured. The nature of offenses against the purity of political life as offenses directly against God has not in recent years been adequately emphasized. Yet we may feel en-

[1] Hooker, *Ecclesiastical Polity*. This is a reprint of the text, but it appears to be corrupt or incomplete, although the meaning is clear enough.

couraged when we compare American political life with the life of the Church in the period preceding the Protestant Reformation. How could a President of the United States be conceived as living a life so debased as that of some of the popes, or others who have held high positions in the Church?

Church and State are much alike in their nature and in their purposes, and it is because they are so much alike that there has been so much conflict between them—conflict of which we shall hear more in the United States in future years than we have in the past. It has been held by some Protestants, like the Lutheran Rothe, that the State in idea is the Church, and that when the perfect State comes it will be the Church. He of course speaks of an idea to be realized in a distant future, but he distinctly states that the Church must decrease and the State increase. This doctrine cannot be elaborated in this place, but it may be asked what need there is of a separate institution for righteousness when the whole of social and individual life and all institutions are permeated with the Christian spirit. We are told, indeed, that there shall be no temple in the New Jerusalem. But certainly we are yet far from this New Jerusalem, and we must work for the extension of the Church, while we at the same time endeavor to instil Christian principles into our entire public as well as private life.

It is true that the main purpose of the State is the religious purpose. Religious laws are the only laws which ought to be enacted. But what are religious laws? Certainly not in the United States laws establishing any particular sectarian views or any theological tenets, in regard to which there may be diversity of opinion, but laws designed to promote the good life. Factory acts, educational laws, laws for the establishment of parks and of playgrounds for children, laws securing honest administration of justice, laws rendering the Courts accessible to the poor as well as the rich—all these are religious laws in the truest sense of the word. The Church can go in many respects far beyond the State. It can place ideals ahead of the State to which the State must gradually approach; it can rebuke and inspire the State; it can quicken the consciences of men, of those who rule and of those who obey. The Church always has the opportunity of doing work neglected by the State, and in particular the dogmas of religion are committed to the Church. Theology in the narrow sense of the term belongs to the Church and not to the modern State. On the other hand, let the Church see to it that all her actions and teachings strengthen and purify the State. Let all Christians see to it that they put as much as possible, not of doctrine or creed into the State constitution, but of Christian life and practice into the activity of the State, working, to be sure, to change the constitution in so far as this may stand in the way of righteousness. The nation must be recognized fully as a Christian nation.

Love of country must show itself in service, in the upbuilding of the institutions of the country. The schools of the country must be nourished. If they lack religious instruction, let the churches supplement the schools on this side. If the conversion of the world is our object, we will not attempt to pull a few out of the world, nor will we so much endeavor to separate our children from the public schools as to make these public schools what they should be. We will establish our centers of religious influences at the seat of State universities and reap the harvest in them which awaits Christian effort. If we have our own separate denominational schools we will see to it that they minister to the entire life of the State, and help, not hinder, public effort.

This serves as illustration, and illustration may be continued indefinitely, but one more illustration may be given to emphasize the thought that real patriotism finds expression in acts, not merely words. The matter of tax-payment is one which in its ethical bearing a Christian cannot neglect. The Apostle Paul commanded Christians to pay tribute, which was a sign of subjugation; only conquered nations pay tribute. How much more should Christians pay their full share of self-imposed taxes, common contributions for common purposes! And remember, he who neglects to pay his fair share, places a heavier burden on some one else, presumably one of the weaker elements in society, as widow or orphan. What would Christ say of tax-dodging coupled with hurrahs for the stars and stripes on the Fourth of July? That is a sort of patriotism to be spewed out of one's mouth.

What in short we especially need, and what the Christian standpoint necessarily carries with it, is emphasis on duties rather than rights. This is a first condition of civic regeneration.

There are now hundreds of various religious sects, and the unity of the various denominations seems remote, even with the best and most earnest efforts. One sort of unity of Christians, however, is found in the State. Men of all denominations act together in the administrative, legislative, and judicial branches of government for the establishment of righteousness. Let this unity be valued at its true worth, let it be cultivated and as much meaning put into it as at any time the circumstances will admit!

CHAPTER IX.
MAKING MEN GOOD BY LAW.

"OF law there can be no less acknowledged, than that her seat is the bosom of God, her voice the harmony of the world: all things in heaven and earth do her homage, the very least as feeling her care, and the greatest as not exempted from her power, both angels and men and creatures of what condition soever, though each in different sort and manner, yet all with uniform consent admiring her as the mother of their peace and joy."—*Hooker's Ecclesiastical Polity, Book I, chapter xvi, p.* 8.

CHAPTER IX.

MAKING MEN GOOD BY LAW.

TWO quotations from widely separated authors will serve as a text for the present chapter. The first is taken from the Rev. Hugh Price Hughes, and is found in his sermon, entitled "National Character Determined by the National Laws," one of the collection making up his book, *Social Christianity*. It reads as follows: "How often we hear it said that 'you cannot make men moral by act of Parliament.' I never heard anybody say that except when he was trying in some way to hinder the kingdom of God. When men try to prevent the advance of the temperance movement and other great moral enterprises, they are very fond of rattling off that sentence. It is supposed to be a reply to moral fanatics; that is to say, to sober and wise patriots. When men glibly tell us that we cannot make men moral by act of Parliament, I should like to know what they mean. They probably do not know themselves. Do they mean that force in itself is no remedy? If so, let them live up to their convictions. But let us not forget that a law is a good deal more than force. An act of Parliament is not mere force, it is educational. It teaches the conscience, it strengthens the conscience, and even the most degraded usually realize that what is illegal is wrong." The second quotation is furnished by Professor Lester F. Ward, and is found in his *Dynamic Sociology*, which, notwithstanding some unfortunate views on religion, is one of the ablest sociological works ever written by an American. The quotation reads as follows: " We may regard all legislation as belonging to one or the other of two general classes: (1) Compulsory legislation ; and (2) attractive legislation. . . . In the department of social forces most of the attempts to control them have thus far been made according to the coercive method ; and this illustrates in a remarkable manner the infantile stage of the science of sociology. We are living in the ' stone age ' of the art of government. We shall not emerge from it until the principle of ' attractive legislation ' is thoroughly understood and applied."

As Mr. Hughes points out, there is a radical difference between modern thinkers, who tell us that you cannot make men good by law, and Moses, one of the greatest, if not the greatest, of all lawgivers, who found the test of national greatness in laws. The ideas of people who

Making Men Good by Law. 181

assert that laws cannot make men good seem to be crude indeed. They evidently suppose that advocates of legislation as an agency of morality wish to accomplish their ends directly and immediately. Let us suppose that we pass a law to the effect that after May 15, 1898, all men in the United States shall be true and upright, ceasing from lying, cheating, begging, and stealing, working diligently with their own hands. We may readily admit that such a law would accomplish nothing. No one in his senses, however, has ever advocated a law decreeing the establishment of goodness. The method to be pursued to make men good by law must be the method of indirectness.

Laws establish the conditions of social life and make social life possible. Now God has made man a social animal, as the wise old teacher, Aristotle, long ago discovered, and it is only in society that man can accomplish his destiny and attain to true moral development. Laws in making possible human society make possible morality. Laws are the basis on which rest the great fundamental social institutions of civilization. Laws are the bulwark of the family, and without laws any amount of preaching cannot preserve the family intact as a social institution. The basis of the family must be something stronger than mere exhortation. Let the laws become weak and inadequate, and fail to protect the family against the assaults of evil forces constantly at work, and divorces multiply, and Mormonism becomes rampant, as we know but too well in the United States, where the importance of law has been so little understood. It goes without saying that teaching and preaching are required to make the family what it should be, but it is asserted without hesitation that this teaching and this preaching cannot be successful unless they rest upon an adequate legal foundation.

Laws are required to make person and property secure, and to enable men to lead their lives in peace, free from the assaults of transgressors. So important is legal security—the guaranty of right against successful attack—that one of the great jurists of this century, Professor Rudolph von Jhering, says that it is a condition of the development of national character. History seems to offer abundant confirmation of this dictum. Subjects of an unprincipled despotism, like the Turks, always become mean and contemptible, servile and tyrannical in turn. Manly character, free and independent, can be developed only in countries where law, suitably enforced, establishes secure conditions of social life.

The laws establish and regulate the conditions

Making Men Good by Law. 183

of industrial life. They give us a certain moral level of competition. What was accomplished by individual effort for the abolition of slavery? We may reply, practically nothing, except in so far as individual effort worked through laws and government. The strong arm of the law abolished slavery, and that alone could abolish it. Competition has continued to operate under freedom as it did under slavery, but it operates on a higher moral plane. Surely much individual effort, much teaching and preaching, are required to make men good who live in the United States, even with slavery abolished, but the law has established a fundamental condition of true morality and goodness.

One function of individual effort and of voluntary combinations of individuals in society must be to arouse public opinion to public evils sufficiently to secure the passage of laws, with satisfactory arrangements for their enforcement. Mr. Hughes tells us that the factory acts of England produced a moral revolution in the manufacturing district called the "Black Country." He uses these words: "In many parts of England women and children were degraded beyond expression, and because a national conscience embodied these protective acts in the statute books of this country, the whole moral condition of vast masses of the people has been entirely changed." The experience of the United States in banking is especially instructive in this connection. The old State Banking laws before our late war were calculated to make banking a disreputable and immoral business. It can scarcely be said that in our early history banking as frequently conducted was an honest business. The legal conditions were too unfavorable, and they directly invited men to cheat and swindle. Whatever criticisms we may pass upon our present banking system, it must be said it is much more favorable to morality, because the laws upon which it rests are honest in purpose and the administrative machinery for their enforcement is adequate. Comparatively speaking, there has been very little dishonesty connected with our National Banks. Few businesses in the country have been so safe, and the law has laid a very heavy hand on transgressors of business morality in the National Banking business.

It ought not to be necessary to mention educational institutions in this connection. It was surprising to read the statement in a religious paper not long ago that legislation could do nothing for the Negroes, that they must look to education and not to legislation. The basis of successful popular education is legislation, and must be legislation.

Making Men Good by Law. 185

Education must be regarded as part of the moral development of man, for the life of man cannot arbitrarily be divided into parts, because the physical, mental, and ethical departments of life are most closely related. Educational institutions furnish an opportunity, even without direct religious instruction, for a teacher to operate directly upon the character of the pupil, and the teachers of the country, take them as a whole, are a morally superior class of citizens. How many hundreds of thousands of men and women of the United States have to thank teachers in public schools for some of the best influences which have entered into their lives!

These general considerations ought to be sufficient to show the close connection of law with morality in the educational sphere of social life; but we may take a narrower, more special view of the subject. Christians believe in reading the Bible, and think that this practice helps to make men better.[1] Universal and compulsory education established by law renders the Bible accessible to all, and we may say that the law is thus indirectly a means of grace, to use the technical religious expression. A recent annual report of

---

[1] In the baptism of children in the Methodist Episcopal Church the minister admonishes the parents or guardians that it is their part and duty to see that their children *read* the Holy Scriptures.

the American Bible Society pointed out widespread illiteracy in the United States as one of the obstacles most difficult to overcome in its beneficent activity, and suggested the passage of laws to secure at least a minimum amount of education to every child.

The penal law and reformatory institutions bring to mind another kind of beneficent activity of legislation. The moral education and value of penal law is remarkable. Missionary workers among the poorer and more ignorant masses often tell us that positive statute law furnishes millions of human beings with nearly all their ideas of morality. It is important, on the one hand, to carry forward this educational work of the law; and, on the other, to educate men morally so that their ideas of right and wrong may not be bounded by legality. While it is true that ideas of right and wrong ought to go much further than is possible for law, it is a gain when positive law can re-enforce the requirements of ethics, giving them a firmer and securer existence. When we look back upon the past development of mankind we must admit that the moral progress of the human race has been largely due to law.

Reformatory institutions established by law have shown their power to reform and improve the morally defective classes of the community.

If reformatory institutions do not make men better, it shows that there is something radically wrong in them, and it must be confessed that such is too often the case with our jails, prisons, and penitentiaries. When, however, the Elmira Reformatory, of Elmira, N. Y., a legal institution, is able to report that eighty per cent of those who leave its gates are permanently reformed, it is difficult to see with what propriety it can be said that you cannot make men good by law.

Anti-poverty has been so associated with a particular sect of social reformers that one hesitates to use the word, yet it is a good one, and the law has done much and is still doing much to lessen if not to abolish poverty, especially in its acute form of pauperism. Christians have ever held that one of the chief functions of the State is the elevation of the weaker members of the community. A reform and improvement of the Poor Law of England in 1834 is generally believed to have greatly lessened pauperism, and although this law is not all that it ought to be, there can be no doubt that this claim for it is warranted by the facts.[1] Still better Poor Laws in German cities like Leipzig, Berlin, and Elberfeld have greatly lessened pauperism, and brought

[1] While the population nearly doubled, the number of persons in receipt of public relief decreased one third.

into helpful connection the strong and the weak. Now to diminish poverty and pauperism means to help men become moral, and if this diminution takes place by law, these men have been made good by statute. We often talk about the classes of men whom Christ reached, and about the common people who heard Him gladly, but it does not seem to have been pointed out that Christ did not reach paupers. Christ converted poor people, and notorious sinners adhered to Him. We read of at least a few rich and cultured persons who listened to the words of Christ, and who were among His early followers, but not of one pauper. All experienced workers among the various defective classes in the community will tell us that in many respects the prospects of a highway robber for a future honorable and useful life are much better than those of a confirmed pauper.

The words quoted above from Professor Ward's *Dynamic Sociology* supplement the preceding remarks. Legislation has accomplished something, statutes do help to make men good; but, as Professor Ward justly remarks, practical sociology is still in the stone age. Laws are chiefly negative, repressive, and mandatory, whereas they ought to be attractive and persuasive as well. Undoubtedly positive legislation is more difficult than negative; but when

Making Men Good by Law. 189

men earnestly give their thoughts to the improvement of their fellows, and study sociology deeply, it will be found practicable to develop a great body of attractive laws. We have followed too exclusively the law of Rome, and have neglected to develop the excellent features which can be found in other legal systems like the Greek and Teutonic, and especially the Mosaic. The Roman law is undoubtedly one of the greatest products of the mind of man, and yet it is extremely imperfect, and some of its weaknesses were at least partially responsible for the downfall of Rome. The Roman law was negative and repressive, and emphasized rights rather than duties, especially so as far as property was concerned, and strengthened tendencies toward plutocracy, which divided population into a few very rich and a vast majority of poor people and paupers. Some beginnings of attractive and persuasive legislation already exist, and perhaps chief among them rank the modern public-school systems. Rewards for meritorious conduct are not unknown. We read occasionally of medals and prizes awarded in the Post Office Department for excellent work, of medals granted to policemen and firemen for courageous conduct, of honors conferred upon those in the Life Saving Service who have hazarded their own lives for others. European countries have other incitements to virtue and patriotic conduct. Men who have rendered distinguished service of any kind in Germany and in England may be raised to the peerage, and they may be rewarded even with large grants of land and money. Monuments are erected to commemorate worthy deeds and distinguished services.

Many things which are practicable in aristocratic European countries are out of the question in the United States, and it remains for us to develop a system of rewards to take the place of decorations, titles, and patents of nobility. We Americans instinctively feel that we ought to honor and reward men who have distinguished themselves for their services to humanity in general or to their country in particular. This is why we elected General Grant President of the United States. He was, possibly, not the best man for that place, and it was not, perhaps, the best kind of reward, but we felt that we must do some great thing for him, so we elected him President twice by overwhelming majorities, and many of us were even inclined to trample on tradition and elect him a third time.

CHAPTER X.
INADEQUACY OF PRIVATE PHILAN-
THROPY FOR SOCIAL REFORM.

" A SHORT time ago I went down to the Pottery district, and was told of the unspeakably degraded condition in which men, women, and children lived before the law of England protected the weak against the greedy and the strong; and I say that when Lord Shaftesbury, as a devout believer in the Lord Jesus Christ, persuaded this country—amid the opposition of John Bright and a great many sincere friends of the people, who did not understand the bearings of the question—to decide that all over England the weak and defenseless should be protected by these acts, he did more to establish the kingdom of Jesus Christ than if he had merely spent his time in preaching thousands of what my critic would call Gospel sermons."—*Rev. Hugh Price Hughes, M.A., Social Christianity, p. 28.*

CHAPTER X.

INADEQUACY OF PRIVATE PHILANTHROPY FOR SOCIAL REFORM.

WISE words were those uttered two thousand years ago : " When thou doest thine alms, do not sound a trumpet before thee, as the hypocrites do in the synagogues and in the streets, that they may have glory of men." It cannot be said that private philanthropy has always obeyed this scriptural injunction. Especially is it true in our day that the achievements of private philanthropy are heralded abroad with trumpets, and all men are called upon to behold the deeds of private philanthropy with admiration. It has thus happened that the possibilities of private philanthropy have been exaggerated, and its proper place as a social agency has been misconceived. Private philanthropy plays an essential rôle in all higher civilization, and when it is modest and unassuming, and deprecates all sounding of trumpets, it is truly a glorious thing. It is, however, spasmodic, irregular, and insufficient for social reform. It is, socially considered, an auxiliary, a subordinate. Social reform must be accomplished chiefly by established, regularly working institutions, served by individual effort and strengthened by private philanthropy.

The limitations and true functions of private philanthropy may be better understood if we consider it in relation to certain lines of social work. It would seem that charitable relief is the sphere of all others for private effort, yet it may be seriously questioned whether individual attempts to relieve pauperism have not done more harm than good. This is true beyond all question so far as almsgiving is concerned. Ever since the modern era of charities began we have been trying to correct the evils of private philanthropy as well as of public effort in this sphere of social activity. Moreover, the evils connected with unwise giving to alleviate poverty must be corrected with the aid of law and public institutions.

Let us turn our attention to education. Private philanthropy endeavored to provide educational facilities for all sorts and conditions of men, and this effort was continued for centuries with the aid of the Church. With what success, however, did it meet? While it cannot be said that nothing was achieved, it must be acknowledged that what was accomplished was small indeed as compared with the achievements of

Inadequacy of Philanthropy. 195

public schools. The State has done what individual effort, alone and unaided, could never accomplish—it has rendered education universal. Probably the experience of no country is more instructive than that of England, because there private individuals, aided by the Church, were intrusted with the duty of providing educational facilities for the nation, and during several hundred years had a fair opportunity to show what could be accomplished in this way. Twenty-five years ago, however, the State undertook to establish an educational system designed to reach every child in England; and in this brief period the State has made more progress than was made by private philanthropy in three centuries. The efforts of despised politicians were incomparably more fruitful in proportion to the expenditure of energy than the sacrifices and exertions of philanthropists.

The question may be raised whether independent private effort to furnish educational facilities does not at present accomplish more harm than good. The author has had abundant opportunity for observation, and while there are many exceptions, and brilliant exceptions, too, he asserts without hesitation that the education furnished by private schools is mostly inferior in quality and, taking it all in all, decidedly below the level established by public schools. As a rule, private schools lack the first condition of success, which is the power to establish discipline, because they are too dependent upon those who patronize them. This is not all, however. Private schools divert energy and attention from public schools, and tend to make the latter poorer than they would otherwise be. Private philanthropy, as represented by great educational societies in England, was opposed to State education. It was an obstacle which had to be overcome.

The author often thinks of the labors of the late lamented Charles Loring Brace, the head of the Children's Aid Society in New York. He established schools for poor children, and was at length able, with the support of private philanthropy, to provide educational facilities for several thousand destitute children. When, however, his work was at the height of its success, some fourteen thousand children were turned away from the doors of the public schools because there was no room for them. To anyone who knows the amount of energy required to support properly a few private industrial schools like those which Mr. Brace established, it can scarcely appear doubtful that the same amount of effort and private philanthropy expended in the improvement of the public schools would have prevented the disgraceful turning away of children from their doors, and would have improved very appreciably the entire public-school system of the city, thus benefiting the hundreds of thousands who attend these schools. This truth seems to be perceived, because it is now proposed to amalgamate these schools with the public schools of New York. The main point which the author has in mind is well brought out by a writer of much insight, who describes the probable result as "greater watchfulness on the part of the workers in such organizations as the Children's Aid Society, to the end that the public schools may now completely fill the requirements of the present day."[1]

Probably there are no two men in the United States whose judgment concerning the education both of the Negroes and of the whites in our Southern States deserves more consideration than Hon. J. L. M. Curry and Dr. A. D. Mayo. They have both recently felt called upon to give emphatic warning against reliance on private schools and the dangerous tendency to concentrate attention and beneficence on these schools rather than on the public schools, which are the chief thing. The following words are quoted from Dr. Mayo, and are unreservedly indorsed by Mr. Curry: "It is high time that we under-

[1] Dr. Albert Shaw in his article, "The Higher Life of New York City," in *The Outlook*, January 25, 1896.

stood that the one agency on which the Negroes and nine tenths of the white people in the South must rely for elementary instruction and training is the American common school. The attempt to educate two millions of colored and three millions of white American children in the South by passing around the hat in the North; sending driblets of money and barrels of supplies to encourage anybody and everybody to open a little useless private school; . . . all this, and a great deal more that is still going on among us, with of course the usual exceptions, has had its day and done its work. The only reliable method of directly helping the elementary department of Southern education is that our churches and benevolent people put themselves in touch with the common-school authorities in all the dark places, urging even their poorer people to do more, as they can do more, than at present. The thousand dollars from Boston that keeps alive a little private or denominational school in a Southern neighborhood, if properly applied, would give two additional months, better teaching and better housing, to all the children, and unite their people as in no other way." [1]

Sanitary reforms are among the most beneficent and important social reforms demanded at

[1] The Education of the Negro," by Hon. J. L. M. Curry. *American Magazine of Civics*, February, 1896.

Inadequacy of Philanthropy. 199

the present time. When we touch upon sanitary reforms, however, we find that individual effort can accomplish almost nothing, except in so far as it aids and supports public authority by helpful co-operation. The experience of cities in Europe and America is most instructive. Public authority in Chicago diminished the percentage of deaths in proportion to population by thirty per cent by important sanitary arrangements. The Mayor of Chicago, in his annual message of April 1890, says that the death rate of the city in 1889 was 17.49 to the thousand, and that this lowered death rate was "due mainly to the extension of the sewer system, in conjunction with the vigilance of the Department of Health. Through the efficiency of the corps of factory and tenement-house inspectors, the sanitary police, and others, nearly eighteen thousand official visitations and notices combined have been made and served for the purpose of correcting various violations of the health laws."

Thousands of lives are saved every year in Liverpool, London, and Glasgow by the improved conditions of life introduced by public authority, which public authority alone could introduce; and sanitary reforms inaugurated in Berlin a few years ago, under the auspices of Professor Virchow, one of the leading scientists of the world, have already saved hundreds of thousands of lives.

The reader must reflect carefully upon what this means. It does not mean merely fewer deaths, but less illness, greater strength and robustness, for the population as a whole, consequently a greater capacity for self-support and self-help of every kind, less pauperism, fewer dependent widows and orphans. We may contrast what public authority has accomplished in sanitary reform with the achievements of private philanthropy in the housing of the poor in cities, both in this country and abroad, but especially in this country.

The need of improved dwellings for the poor was pointed out in New York city a generation ago, and the appeal to private philanthropy to take up the work of tenement-house reform has from that time to this been uninterrupted. Wealthy Christians in particular have been entreated and implored to enter this work, and all sorts of considerations have been urged why they should take it up. The appeal has been to self-interest as well as to generosity. There is more than one professed Christian in New York city whose resources are sufficient, alone and unaided, to renovate the tenement houses of New York city. Yet what has private philanthropy accomplished? There are a few model tenements in New York and Brooklyn, but in proportion to the need of the people they are almost less than a drop in the bucket. It may be said without hesitation that a single sanitary law, even with imperfect means of administration, has accomplished more for the tenement-house population than all the achievements of private philanthropy in a generation.

Compare also the following, quoted from *St. Andrew's Cross*, February, 1896: "Richard Watson Gilder, the editor of the *Century*, who last year served his city as the Chairman of the New York Tenement-House Commission, says, as a result of observation upon a recent trip abroad, that the European slums are fast disappearing under the enforcement of rigid sanitary laws. Many buildings, which were the breeding places of disease in the Whitechapel district of London, have been torn down and replaced by clean, wholesome houses, properly equipped with all sanitary appliances, and owned and controlled by the municipality." We have no reason to believe that private effort alone could in ten thousand years have accomplished this result. On the other hand, we can never secure laws of this kind without private effort, and in the United States, at least, the laws once secured cannot be enforced without a vast amount of determined and probably also organized private effort.

We can also see in this connection how the

success and possibilities of private philanthropy are overrated. A most estimable gentleman in Brooklyn has established some model tenements. The example which he has set has had comparatively little influence; these model tenements are reaching perhaps a few hundred people; they furnish the subject of numerous articles, attention is again and again called to them, and honors are conferred upon the man who established them. Far be it from the author to detract from the praise which is his due, yet the fact ought to be emphasized that relatively speaking we can hardly say that anything has been done toward the solution of the problem. Attention is fixed upon the few reached by such efforts, but the millions unreached are forgotten. On the other hand, when law and administration reach beneficially a million people, it is all taken for granted as a mere matter of course, and it is not thought worth while to call attention to blessings conferred by government.

This is still more plainly seen in the educational field. It is a noble spectacle to see the people of New York State, rich and poor alike, voluntarily tax themselves seventeen millions of dollars a year for education; yet this achievement of self-government is scarcely noticed, whereas the gift of a few millions by a private man, who has left more than he can possibly need, is heralded from Dan to Beersheba, and cannot be admired sufficiently. We are not to detract from the praise we owe the rich man, but we should not lose a proper sense of proportion.

Industrial reforms ought to be carefully examined in order to determine the limits and functions of legislation and administration on the one hand, and of private philanthropy on the other. Child labor has been a great and growing evil in this and other countries. Attention has been called to it in the press and in the pulpit. Thousands—perhaps hundreds of thousands—of sermons and editorials have appealed to the individual to abate the evils of child labor. The nature of these evils has been explained again and again. Child labor in hundreds of thousands of cases destroys mind, body, and soul. When it was at its worst in England, physicians testified that the generation growing up was stunted in body and weak in intellect, and the moral evils were patent to all observers. Nevertheless it may it be said without fear of contradiction from any well-informed and honest person that private philanthropy, alone and unaided, accomplished simply nothing. While eloquent sermons were preached, moving editorials penned, and even poems like Mrs. Browning's " Cry of the Children " written the evil of child labor increased without interruption until the strong arm of the law interfered, and owing to legislation and administration the worst evils have disappeared in England, and have been greatly lessened in States like Massachusetts.

Sunday labor brings us to another topic of industrial importance. Private philanthropy is so strongly re-enforced by religion when it attempts to lessen the amount of Sunday toil that perhaps something appreciable can be accomplished. Nevertheless, the evil of needless Sunday toil can as a whole be abolished only by legislation. We may take up many other industrial reforms, and we will find that as a matter of fact private philanthropy has not accomplished the change needed; and if we analyze industrial phenomena, we ascertain that it never can secure the desired result. The reason is that men are bound together in industrial life by the law of social solidarity, and within certain narrow limits what one does the others must do, or become bankrupt. This gives the worst men in the community an enormous power, unless they are restrained by law. If one barber out of twenty keeps open his barber shop on Sunday, the temptation for the other nineteen is stronger because they are competitors, and they fear they will lose a part of their regular business. Among the other nineteen we shall find at least one who will follow the example of the least scrupulous among the twenty. We shall then have two whose barber

Inadequacy of Philanthropy. 205

shops are open on Sunday, and the temptation to the other eighteen becomes still stronger, and at least another will yield quickly. Thus the temptation to do business on Sunday will continually increase, until the twentieth man will find himself confronted with the alternative of keeping his shop open on Sunday or quitting business. It is thus that an entire trade may become demoralized. Barbers have been known to raise money to secure the passage of a city ordinance closing barber shops, and the Sunday closing of barber shops has been advocated by the national organization of the barbers and thus become a live question in our cities. The author has himself heard a photographer in New York say that he would gladly give one hundred dollars to have a law passed closing all the photographic galleries in the city on Sunday, in order that he might close his without becoming a bankrupt. We have in all this what the author has called *the problem of the twentieth man.*

The great lines of social reform must be the concern of agencies which work steadily and persistently, and the support of which does not depend upon the life of any individual or on the vicissitudes of individual fortune. These are, however, always individual cases which require individual treatment, and they furnish the chief field for private effort and generosity. A private individual may discover a poor boy with a great talent for art and educate him, and thus confer a benefit upon the community.

There are always many persons temporarily in need and distress who can be better assisted quietly by private philanthropy, and in fact can only be relieved by such philanthropy. There is also abundant opportunity for individual effort of every kind in assisting in improving the action of public agencies. The administration of law with us is imperfect, and is so arranged that it often fails to protect the poorer members of the community. The Chicago Bureau of Justice illustrates the kind of effort needed to help poor people protect their rights. It is organized by private effort, its very efficient secretary is a competent lawyer, and it undertakes to secure justice for those who are comparatively helpless, especially for wage-earning women. With small outlay it has benefited thousands directly, and tens of thousands indirectly, because it is feared by unscrupulous oppressors. It endeavors, however, not merely to render the machinery of law available to all, but it attempts also to improve this machinery, so that it may be less difficult for the ordinary man to secure his rights.[1]

[1] The annual reports of this society are most instructive. For these reports and other information the reader should apply to

The Elberfeld system of poor relief is an excellent model, because it combines so admirably private and public agencies. Poor relief was administered by the city for a time unsuccessfully, and it was then turned over by the city to the churches and private effort combined, but that experiment did not work well, and finally the city again took charge of poor relief, but in such a manner as to secure the active co-operation of the best private citizens.

It was thus that the so-called Elberfeld system of poor relief was established. It means the organization of charities by public authorities, their unification through the municipality, and their general supervision by regular officials ; but these are assisted by some hundreds of private citizens who serve as friendly visitors. Every condition of success is thus present. The evils of giving are reduced to a minimum, the benefits of giving increased, and pauperism is greatly lessened. It is not said that this precise system can

Joseph W. Errant, Esq., Agent and Attorney, Rooms 718 and 719, Garden City Block, Randolph Street and Fifth Avenue, Chicago, Ill. The New Century Club of Philadelphia has organized a Committee on Legal Protection for workingwomen, and furnishes advice, court charges, and counsel free to women who work for their living, and are too poor or uninformed of legal methods to protect themselves. Information regarding methods, etc., can be obtained from Mrs. S. C. F. Hallowell, Chairman, 124 South Twelfth Street, Philadelphia, Pa.

be transplanted to our shores, but it is asserted without hesitation that the harmonious co-operation of public authority and private effort is needed to secure the best results.

Let no one say that the office of private philanthropy is not sufficiently large. Without it, nothing can be accomplished. In a vast field it alone has undisputed sway, and in this field no willing worker need lack opportunity for usefulness, and no one with surplus wealth can say that the calls upon him will not be sufficiently large, even if public activity has an enlarged scope. Moreover, private philanthropy must precede legislation and make it possible, and it must enlighten public opinion, or good laws cannot be enforced. Sanitary reform and factory acts have been brought about by the efforts of philanthropists. What is wanted is to direct philanthropy into proper channels, in order that thus it may accomplish the greatest good of which it is capable.

CHAPTER XI.
OUR EARNINGS.

"IT is impossible to conclude, of any given mass of acquired wealth, merely by the fact of its existence, whether it signifies good or evil to the nation in the midst of which it exists. Its real value depends on the moral sign attached to it just as sternly as that of a mathematical quantity depends on the algebraical sign attached to it. Any given accumulation of commercial wealth may be indicative, on the one hand, of faithful industries, progressive energies, and productive ingenuities; or, on the other, it may be indicative of mortal luxury, merciless tyranny, ruinous chicane. Some treasures are heavy with human tears, as an ill-stored harvest with untimely rain; and some gold is brighter in sunshine than it is in substance."—*Ruskin, Unto This Last, ii.*

CHAPTER XI.

OUR EARNINGS.

BY the ancients, both among the Jews and among other highly civilized nations, much has been written on the acquisition of wealth. The best given us by the Jews on this subject is naturally found in the Bible, and perhaps nothing better has been given us by the wise men of old of other nations than is found in the writings of Plato and Aristotle. There is singular unanimity on the part of these ancient writers in regard to many fundamental points which touch the acquisition of wealth. Moreover, there is general harmony on the part of the fathers of the Church and their successors up to modern times, as well as of wise political philosophers of all ages, touching the fundamental principles involved in the acquisition of wealth. John Wesley, in his sermon on "The Use of Money,"[1] presents leading principles clearly which will guide us wisely if simply elaborated so that they may be made applicable to our new times. Our age is doubtless one of progress, but the careful student can

[1] Wesley, *Sermons*, vol. i, pp. 444-448.

scarcely fail to see, in particulars, retrogression. There hardly seems to be dominant as clear ideas and as sound ideas touching our earnings as those which have been current in past ages.

If we open our Bibles and examine what the various writers in the Bible have said concerning the acquisition of wealth,.one of the first things which must strike us is the praise of moderation. The greatest weight is attached to this, and it is made, indeed, a duty of high rank. The utterances of the Bible on this point agree in the main with the teachings of Plato and Aristotle. While the various bodies of Christians claim that the Bible gives sufficient guidance in all affairs of life, all enlightened persons are glad to receive subsidiary aid from other writers, and it may be well to give a short space to the ideas of the great social philosophers who have just been named.

Plato states that the very rich man can hardly be a very good man, and he gives certain reasons for his view. He says that there are different sources of acquisition, those which are just and those which are unjust, and that he who derives riches from both sources indifferently, will gain more than double the wealth of him who derives his riches from just sources only. The bad man has, moreover, an advantage, Plato claims, in the expenditure of money, spending only half as much as the good man. "The sums," says he, "which are expended neither honorably nor disgracefully are only half as great as those which are expended honorably and on honorable purposes." It thus happens, according to Plato, that the good man cannot be wealthier than the bad man. On the other hand, "The utterly bad man is in general profligate and therefore very poor; while he who spends on noble objects and acquires wealth by just means only can hardly be remarkable for riches, any more than he can be very poor."[1] Plato again and again comes back to the position that the end of the state is the production of men and not of wealth, and that moderation secures the best results.

Aristotle views the subject in its broader aspects, and gives special attention to the political effects of accumulations which go beyond a moderate competence. He fears poverty, which he claims leads to revolutions; but he regards great wealth as even more destructive. He dreads what he styles "the encroachments of the rich."[2] In another place Aristotle uses these words: "Those who have too much of the goods of fortune, strength, health, friends, and the like, are neither willing nor able to submit to authority. The evil begins at home: for when they are boys, by reason of the luxury in which they are brought

[1] Jewett's *Plato*, vol. v, p. 125.
[2] Jewett's *Politics of Aristotle*, pp. 131, 145.

up, they never learn even at school the habit of obedience. On the other hand, the very poor who are in the opposite extreme are too degraded. . . . Thus arises a city, not of freemen, but of masters and slaves, the one despising, the other envying."[1] Aristotle also points out the danger that the cares of property will keep men from attending to public business.[2]

The ideal of the Bible with respect to earnings is given in Agur's prayer: "Give me neither poverty nor riches; feed me with food convenient for me: lest I be full, and deny thee, and say, Who is the Lord? or lest I be poor, and steal, and take the name of my God in vain."[3] In another chapter in Proverbs we read these words: "He that tilleth his land shall have plenty of bread. . . . A faithful man shall abound with blessings: but he that maketh haste to be rich shall not be innocent [Revised Version, "unpunished"]. . . . He that hasteth to be rich hath an evil eye, and considereth not that poverty shall come upon him."[4]

When we turn from the Old to the New Testament, we find the same ideas expressed with equal emphasis. We remember what our Saviour said about the difficulty with which a rich man could enter into the kingdom of Heaven. St.

[1] Jewett's *Politics of Aristotle*, p. 127.   [2] *Ibid.*, pp. 119, 120.
[3] Proverbs xxx, 8, 9.   [4] Proverbs xxviii, 19, 20, 22.

Paul utters these well-known words: "But they that will be rich fall into temptation and a snare, and into many foolish and hurtful lusts, which drown men in destruction and perdition. For the love of money is the root of all evil."[1]

This moderation, which is the ideal, means negatively an avoidance of hurtful desires for large acquisitions and of those wrong practices which spring out of the bad disposition. But positively it means diligence, thrift, and all rightful efforts to acquire a competence. The Bible, and the other writings which have been quoted, all insist upon this positive aspect of the ideal. The dangers of poverty are pointed out. Aristotle speaks of the temptation to crime and revolution which poverty carries with it. Agur's prayer points to the danger that poverty may lead to a denial of God. St. Paul admonishes Christians to be diligent in business, not slothful. Apart from the public dangers which attend poverty, other evils follow from a lack of diligence and foresight and the self-denial involved in frugality. First, we must notice that if we do not exert ourselves to acquire the things needful, there is danger that we may become a burden upon others. Second, we must remember that without these efforts which are commended to acquire a moderate supply of material goods, we

[1] 1 Timothy vi, 9, 10.

shall not have a surplus ourselves to do for those who need our help. Of course, there will ever be those who, in spite of all they can do, through accident, infirmity, etc., will require help, and provision must be made for these; and it is no reproach to these to accept gratefully the help cheerfully proffered.

Moreover, moderation leads to contentment, which is highly prized. While making all due effort to improve our condition, we are at the same time enjoined to be content with what we have.

If space were not too limited, a cloud of witnesses could be quoted, all of them emphasizing again and again the dangers of wealth and the importance in all particulars of moderation in our efforts to acquire wealth. As it is, we must be content with only one or two quotations. Bishop Wilson, who is quoted approvingly by Matthew Arnold,[1] uses these words: " Riches are almost always abused without a very extraordinary grace." Professor Bruce, in his *Kingdom of God*, expresses himself as follows: " Possession, or wealth, in every form, is conservative, cautious, slow in sympathy, and languid in support; whether it be the intellectual wealth of knowledge, or the moral wealth of character, or the material wealth of outward property. The rôle

[1] *Culture and Anarchy*, p. 167.

Our Earnings. 217

of the rich in wisdom, wealth, or gold, is not that of the ardent pioneer, but of the tardy patriot; so they miss the glory of martyrdom and also its pain. Their place in the history of the kingdom is a very mean one; in the more heroic phases of that history they are mainly conspicuous by their absence."[1] It will be noticed that he speaks of the "wise" much as Christ does. In another place he says: "The wise espouse no cause when it is new."[2] Those familiar with our higher institutes of learning know what a large measure of truth there still is in this assertion concerning the conservatism of those who have much book learning.[3]

The reasons for this ideal of moderation in wealth acquisition have been already expressly stated or implied. One of the weightiest is that craving for wealth turns away attention from higher spiritual things. This is seen with great clearness by Plato, who uses these words: "For there are, in all, three things about which every man has an interest; and the interest about money, when rightly regarded, is the third and last of them; midway comes the interest of the

---
[1] *Kingdom of God*, p. 302.   [2] *Ibid.*, p. 302.
[3] "A learned class will appreciate indeed certain thoughts to which the multitude are indifferent, but not wholly new thoughts, not thoughts foreign to its learning."—Sir J. R. Seeley, *Natural Religion*, p. 103.

body; and, first of all, that of the soul."[1] How strikingly in harmony is this with the thought of the Biblical writers! Christ, Himself, makes special mention of the deceitfulness of riches as one of the causes which hinder the extension of the kingdom.

We notice, also, the dangers to our own mind and body which accompany undue and feverish activity in the acquisition of wealth; likewise the neglect of the bodies, minds, and souls of others, which too frequently attends immoderate efforts in wealth acquisition, and also the neglect of civic duties. When we are bent upon wealth, we employ indifferently the just and unjust sources of its acquisition. Again, it is to be observed that poverty is one of the dangers which threaten those who make haste to be rich. They take undue risks, and frequently lose their all. How many hundreds of thousands of families in this broad land would to-day enjoy a competence, who now live in poverty, had they not made haste to be rich.[2]

A few points must be elaborated further, and

[1] Jewett's *Plato*, p. 126.
[2] An analysis of the causes of failures in business in the United States since 1892 has been made by one of our commercial agencies, and it is alleged that haste to be rich, shown in capital inadequate for the business undertaken, is the chief cause; commercial crisis ranks second; incompetency, third; and fraud, fourth.

we cannot do better than to take them up somewhat in the order in which we find them in Wesley's sermon on "The Use of Money."

Wesley strongly insists upon the importance of diligence and the utmost use of rightful opportunities in wealth acquisition, but he points out the dangers which must be avoided. We ought not to gain money, he tells us, at the expense of our life or of our health; therefore, we should never enter into nor continue in an employment "attended with so hard or so long labor as to impair our constitution." Proper seasons of food and sleep in such proportion as our nature requires must not be neglected. But as we seek occupation under such conditions for ourselves, we must likewise avoid anything which can injure in these particulars our neighbors. Unduly long hours and unhealthful avocations are especially mentioned. Wesley speaks about lead workers, and lead working is still an unhealthful occupation. He also condemns employments dealing with arsenic or other hurtful minerals. As a mere matter of course, it follows from his premises that Sunday work must be avoided, or, in case Sunday work is a necessity, that one day of rest in seven should be secured.

We observe that Wesley treats this subject chiefly from an individual point of view. We must now add the social point of view, for the character of our industrial life has changed essentially since Wesley wrote his sermon. The modern era of competition, based upon division of labor and exchange, is essentially a product of this century, and it gives us social solidarity of such a sort that the individual alone is unable to govern the conditions under which he works and earns his daily bread, or, indeed, acquires a competence. Wesley had in mind, evidently, the man working in a small shop or on a farm, and who could regulate largely the conditions of his toil. We must think of the street-car employee who has to work frequently too many hours a day, and very often seven days in a week, or else lose his occupation. We must remember the army of those who are employed in great factories and manufacturing establishments, and who must toil under conditions which are the same for all, and which are beyond the control of the individual. It is these modern conditions which have given rise to the modern system of factory legislation, prohibiting the toil of very young children, limiting the toil of young persons and women, safeguarding the home, prescribing healthful conditions under which toil must be conducted. All this is entirely in line with Wesley's rules of industrial conduct and a necessary deduction from it.

But one quotation from Wesley is important

because it points to practices which it seems were not unknown in his day, but with the growth of great industry have become far more serious. " We cannot," says Wesley, " consistently, with brotherly love, sell our goods below the market price; we cannot study to ruin our neighbor's trade in order to advance our own; much less can we entice away or receive any of his servants or workmen whom he has need of. None can gain by swallowing up his neighbor's substance without gaining the damnation of hell."[1] The application to current conditions is self-evident. Those competitive methods which increase our own substance at the expense of our neighbor's prosperity are condemned in the strongest terms.

Another strong point made by Wesley, and which is found also in the Discipline of the Methodist Episcopal Church, is that we must not defraud the king (that is to say, the state) of his lawful customs. This is done in many ways at the present time. There are still those who smuggle goods into the country, and it is noticeable that women especially seem to have little

[1] This cannot be applied to legitimate competition so long as we have a competitive system of industry, but it does apply, as Wesley intended it should, to deliberate attempts to break down our rivals and secure a monopoly, partial or complete, for ourselves.

conscience in this matter, their singular deficiency in this respect probably being due to their lack of civic training, and consequently civic consciousness. But this implies, likewise, any withholding of taxes of any sort due to nation, commonwealth, or city; or any traffic which derives a gain from frauds upon the public treasury.

It is furthermore specially noticed that we must not hurt our neighbor by selling him anything which is injurious to him. Spirituous liquors are particularly mentioned, and Wesley's note in regard to the character of the traffic in intoxicating beverages is as clear as anyone could desire. He says that the curse of God rests upon the wealth thereby gained. Food adulterations would come under this same head, and here likewise we see the need of social regulation. The problem of the "twentieth man" again confronts us. One begins to adulterate his food products, and through the force of competition others gradually fall in line until an entire trade is demoralized. The position which is taken in the Discipline of the Methodist Episcopal Church with respect to temperance reform, in which it is stated that it "rests chiefly upon the combined and sanctified influence of the Family, the Church, and the State" is applicable generally to those reforms which have been suggested with respect to our earnings.

CHAPTER XII.
OUR SPENDINGS.

"THE idea of ancient Roman civilization should be reproduced in our day: 'Private expenditures were small, public expenditures large.' We may be simple in our habits although surrounded by wealth; and, by using the more costly appliances in our possession for the general enjoyment, we may realize the Christian idea of a stewardship. This is the tendency which the Church must foster in social life among all classes of its members."—*The Hon. and Rev. W. H. Fremantle, D.D., The World as the Subject of Redemption, p. 346.*

CHAPTER XII.

OUR SPENDINGS.

OUR spendings are closely connected with our earnings. Consumption of wealth is the purpose of acquisition. He who spends without earning is a parasite, a cumberer of the ground, living upon the toil of others. But earning in this case must be understood in a very broad sense and include any useful service. Man does not live by bread alone, but the service to justify consumption ethically must be an individual service. The fact that a person may have acquired wealth by gift, or inheritance, does not justify consumption on any ethical grounds, unless his acquired wealth is attended with personal service.

Individual responsibility is more pronounced in our spendings than in our earnings. We find an established social system into which we are placed, and in our earnings, within certain limits, we must be governed by the social system which exists. The very words " social system " suggest something formed by society and which can be changed only by society. The individual, to produce changes in the social system, must work in and through society. But when, as a result of our efforts within the social system, which exists, we receive certain sums of wealth annually, these sums are largely within our individual control, and we must be held individually responsible for our use of our power to make expenditures.

The supreme law which governs us in our spending is the law of mutual love. "Love thy neighbor as thyself" is a principle which must be applied to this department of our life as to all others. The test question for the individual is this: "Do I, in my spendings—or what we call, in Political Economy, my 'consumption'—show that I love my neighbor equally with myself?"

John Wesley has given the following directions to guide us in our consumption: "If you desire to be a faithful and a wise steward, out of that portion of your Lord's goods which He has for the present lodged in your hands, but with the right of resuming whenever it pleases Him, first, provide things needful for yourself: food to eat, raiment to put on, whatever nature moderately requires for preserving the body in health and strength. Secondly, provide these for your wife, your children, your servants, or any others who pertain to your household. If, when this is done, there be an overplus left, then 'do good to them

Our Spendings. 227

that are of the household of faith.' If there be an overplus still, 'as you have opportunity, do good unto all men.' "[1]

We have here an order of expenditure which is helpful. I must first provide for myself and for my family. And the provision for one's self and the members of one's family includes the training of all our powers and faculties, and the maintenance of our strength. This sometimes involves a large expenditure, as in the case of a musician, an artist, or a scholar. This disproportionate expenditure might seem at first sight selfish and a violation of the principle of mutual love. Considered more carefully, it is not, provided these powers, developed and maintained at their best, are used in social service. There is no power like that of a gifted and thoroughly trained man devoted to the well-being of others. His powers are of indefinitely greater value to society than anything needful for their full cultivation and maintenance. The family must come before others. We proceed from self to larger and larger circles. There are those who would bring a reproach against Christ because in their opinion he had no regard for the family. There is no ground, however, for the supposition that He was wanting in any respect in consideration of those members of the family into which He

[1] *Sermons*, vol. i, p. 447.

was born. While hanging on the cross in intensest agony He was able to think of His mother, and instructed His beloved disciple to care for her as his mother. "When Jesus therefore saw His mother, and the disciple standing by, whom He loved, He saith unto His mother, Woman, behold thy son! Then saith He to the disciple, Behold thy mother! And from that hour that disciple took her unto his own home."[1]

But clearly and unquestionably Christ taught that our circles must expand until the whole world should be included. We should in our spending, so far as may be, have reference to the welfare of the entire world. We must not neglect the family. Families build up nations. We must not neglect the nation, for it is through the nation that humanity is lifted up; but we can never stop short of entire humanity. As it is narrow and hurtful even to the family to confine one's interests to the family, so it is likewise narrow and hurtful even to the nation to restrict one's benevolence to one's own nation. All the nations of the world are our concern. It is a shortsighted and selfish policy of social reformers to denounce foreign missions!

But we must consider our expenditures in the broadest sense. We are not concerned merely with material wealth, but with personal services

[1] John xix, 26, 27.

of every kind, and with all our powers. The talent intrusted to us may be some intellectual gift, or it may be a quantity of material wealth, and the responsibility is as great in the former case as in the latter. All our time is something for the use of which we are equally responsible.

The reason why we should proceed from smaller to larger circles is obvious upon a little reflection. It is in this way that all wants will best be satisfied and that the general welfare will best be promoted. We have only to ask ourselves this question, What would happen if we proceeded in the reverse way? to see clearly that this is true. It requires, indeed, judgment and self-examination to hold a true balance between all the claims upon us. There are those who unduly neglect the narrower circle with which we may begin, but there can be no doubt that the more general fault is of the opposite kind. There is such a thing as family selfishness as well as purely individual selfishness. It is a part of a higher and better civilization to overcome both. Fortunately there are those standing outside the narrower circles of interest who can give themselves entirely to the larger circles.

It is helpful to classify our wants. We make expenditures for necessaries, for conveniences, for comforts, and for ostentation. Such a classification may be sufficient for present purposes. Our consumption will follow along the line of this classification. Necessaries must first be provided. Other things being equal, we must place upon a higher plane the necessaries of others than those things which are to us merely conveniences and comforts. The considerations, however, which we have already adduced will show that often other things are not equal. Conveniences and comforts may be helpful to us in our work, and thus find ample justification. When we come, however, to expenditures for ostentation, for mere show and display, we must draw a sharp line; they are absolutely interdicted by the law of mutual love. We cannot find any justification in ourselves for such expenditures. Any attempted justification when analyzed is found to involve ignorance of the real nature of our acts, or juggling with ourselves. Such expenditures are what we may call, properly, luxuries, and they are condemned, not only by wise political philosophers of all ages, but by the fathers of the Church, with singular unanimity. How can I claim that I love my brother as myself when I see him need the very necessaries of life and expend money for that which contributes in no measure to my real well-being? The whole tone of the Bible, from beginning to end, condemns in the strongest terms anything of the kind. Not only this, but anything of the kind is condemned explicitly in the severest language, over and over again, and it is an entire contradiction to the example which Christ set us in His own life.

A further discrimination may be made between expenditures for exclusive and those for inclusive pleasures. Food and clothing are exclusively consumed. I alone enjoy my consumption of these articles. A house is more inclusive in the satisfactions it affords. It may minister to many. Still another distinction is that between outlays for things which quickly perish and those which endure for a long time. Other things being equal, the expenditures for inclusive pleasures are ethically preferable to those for exclusive pleasures, although many delight in exclusiveness as such, showing a mind the exact opposite of that of Christ. Naturally, also, an expenditure unjustifiable for an object which would yield pleasures but for a moment, might require no justification if it were for an object of enduring value.

It may be worth while to stop for a moment to consider one very lame justification which people frequently use as a salve to conscience in their attempted evasion of social responsibility. It is said that luxury gives employment. Louis XIV, one of the most extravagant kings of

France, said, "When a king makes great outlays, he gives alms." A newspaper writer, speaking of certain extravagant social events which occurred a few years since, used these words: "Murmurs against luxury may be heard among people in straitened circumstances when the lavish expenditures and sumptuous pleasures of great society entertainments are discussed. But such persons are prone to forget that these expenditures that seem so prodigal go in large part to benefit the working people." We cannot consider now all the economic fallacies involved in arguments of this kind. They have been exposed over and over again by able men. It may, however, simply be pointed out that the same expenditure made in behalf of others would give equal employment to labor. Let us take the case of a man who contributes a million dollars for a public building, and contrast it with the case of a man who spends a million dollars on his own private house. Labor has equal employment in both cases, but the benefit of the toil accrues to the public in the one case, and in the other to the selfish enjoyment of an individual. Another comparison: Contrast the expenditure of ten thousand dollars for an evening's entertainment with an expenditure of ten thousand dollars for books for a public library. Labor is alike employed in both cases, but in the second case the enjoyment is more widely diffused and is of a far more enduring character. This attempted justification is precisely on a line with that which people advance for the maintenance of gambling dens and the support of the traffic in intoxicating beverages. As the author writes, there lies before him a long description of a vast brewery; emphasis is laid upon the large employment which it gives to labor both directly and indirectly. Mention is made of the hop raisers in various parts of the country and to the growers of barley. The article closes with the statement that every keg of beer sold by this New York brewery "helps to buy pianos for our farmers' wives and daughters." The late Professor Cairnes, an able and conservative political economist, uses these words concerning the abundant expenditures of the idle rich: "Political economy furnishes no such palliation of unmitigated selfishness. . . . The wealth accumulated by their ancestors, or others, on their behalf, when it is employed as capital, no doubt helps to sustain industry. But what they consume in luxury and idleness is not capital, and helps to sustain nothing but their own unprofitable lives. By all means they must have their rents and interest as it is written in the bond; but let them take their proper place as drones in the hive, gorging at a feast to which they have contributed nothing."[1] The whole of this will not apply to the industrious rich, but what has been said condemns likewise their luxury, which is contrary to the doctrine of stewardship, and violates the law of mutual love.

The principles which are under discussion, however, admit of greater inequalities than one might at first suppose. Needs vary indefinitely. We have the variation found in inequalities of capacities and faculties already mentioned. The differences in expenditures required for the best and harmonious development of all our powers vary immensely. Moreover, apart from personal development, what is necessary to one person may be wanton extravagance to another. A large library, costing thousands of dollars, is a wise consumption for many individuals, although the housing of it, and the care of it, also, involve continuous expenditures. But for the majority, the expenditure for books which is wise is limited, especially since the era of public libraries. Again, the positions which different men occupy cause large variations in justifiable expenditures. A man in public station frequently cannot live in a manner which would be proper for him if his station were a private one. Not only this, but his expenditures in many respects have a public character, and their benefits are widely diffused.

[1] *Some Leading Principles of Political Economy*, pp. 32, 33.

The writer has in mind the president of a university in one city, whose expenditures exceed many times what would be possible for the average mechanic or farmer, and which, nevertheless, are wisely and generously made. Strangers of distinction are entertained and hospitality extended to professors and students. The benefits of a refined and cultivated home are shared by many. The writer has also in mind a household in another city which, in the entertainment of strangers and the extension of hospitality to persons of distinction coming to the city, for years occupied almost a semipublic position. It is altogether fitting and proper that men who have attained distinction on account of their services in art or letters, or on account of their high position in the State, should receive suitable recognition when they visit other parts of their own country or foreign lands. The reader can continue this line of thought for himself. It may be applied to the President of the United States, or an American ambassador at a court of a foreign power. The purpose is to show that while we must draw a line and condemn most strongly the wanton luxury of our period, we must make discriminations; above all things, we must never be animated by petty envy and jealousy. Yet there never was a time for plainer speaking on this subject. Now is the time for prophets to arise with a message: "Thou art the man;" and to bring home to us our shortcomings with respect to our wealth consumption. Yet it is not merely the rich who stand condemned, but the disposition which is found in all social classes, and which expresses itself now in one way and now in another. The disease is, indeed, widespread.

The discrimination which has already been made suggests other distinctions which must be borne in mind. We cannot at all place upon the same plane private and public expenditures. Expenditures for private galleries, libraries, and mansions, which must be condemned without reservation, are amply justified when made for public purposes. Millions of dollars expended for public galleries of art are justified because their benefits extend to countless thousands, and continue for generations. The large diffusion of benefits, the satisfaction and the joy in fine architecture, will justify grand public buildings. Such expenditure as this tends to elevate the public life. It will naturally follow, from what is said, that the author cannot join in the condemnation of the expenditure of millions for a magnificent church or a great cathedral, provided always that the structure is to be administered for the benefit of the masses, and not for the private enjoyment of the few. If the structure is to be, as it is asserted some church buildings are, a sort of clubhouse for millionaires, then it cannot be approved from an ethical standpoint. But if it is to be a grand architectural work for the spiritual uplifting of men, the expenditure is a wise one.

Another line of thought is suggested by improvements in wealth production. As things become cheaper their enjoyment may become more widely diffused, and that which was a luxury at one time can no longer be placed in this category at present. This process will continue indefinitely. What we condemn is not the enjoyment of what nature and society provide; asceticism finds no sanction in this book. The main point is the limitation of resources, or, as some one has said, that there is not enough material wealth to go round and satisfy all needs. When we spend large sums for what is rare and costly, we lessen our power to satisfy more urgent needs of others; but when rare and costly things become common, the consumption of them must be judged differently.

What has just been stated suggests another excuse which men urge to justify themselves in self-indulgence. It is said that it is the luxury of the rich which encourages improvements, and thus that such consumption finds justification. A little careful reflection, however, will show within what narrow limits this is true. Moreover, the justifiable inequality of which we have spoken, and the large public consumption for the satisfaction of social needs already mentioned, together with other forces continuously operating, will be quite sufficient to bring about improvements; or, should there be any slight loss in this one particular, it would be counterbalanced by an immense gain in other respects.

Different tests have been proposed to determine what may be justified in way of personal expenditure, and what we must condemn. A person who examines himself conscientiously in this regard cannot be very seriously perplexed, and at any rate is not likely to spend too much upon himself. Occasionally a conscientious person will spend even too little upon himself because he fails to appreciate the importance of the cultivation and maintenance of all that he has within himself.

We have heard much lately about the difficulties of giving, and these have been so strangely magnified as to suggest the thought that we have to do with another false plea for the evasion of social responsibility. A highly esteemed religious periodical quoted a millionaire approvingly who used these words: "Let anyone attempt to give away one hundred thousand dollars a year, and do good, not harm, in the giving, and he will find that he has undertaken a task of much greater

Our Spendings. 239

difficulty than the making of one hundred thousand dollars a year." This utterance was spoken of as the "truth, patent and appalling." A short time previously, however, this same periodical printed an appeal for a gift of one hundred thousand dollars for an institution which it was claimed was doing admirable work; and shortly afterward an editorial appeared, entitled "Three Urgent Calls."

A bishop in one of our Southern States recently said in an address: "One of the two or three enormously and absurdly rich men in the country—dead now, and enjoying a little rest I hope—said to me once, 'I envy you.' 'Envy me?' I asked. 'Yes; you are a free man, your own master, and doing and saying hopeful things to people every day; and I am like a blind horse in a bark-mill, tramping the same monotonous path round the safe that contains the deeds and securities.'" The bishop offered to help him bear his burden. He knew exactly where five millions would found a university, doing enormous good; where another million would endow ten missionary bishoprics; where five millions more could be used advantageously toward the instruction and Christianizing of seven million Negroes. The bishop also mentioned places where several other millions could be used; but, although the rich man would still have been struggling under a burden of millions, he declined the proposal.

From what the writer knows of the bishop, and of his situation, he has no doubt that all these millions could have been employed to good advantage in the ways pointed out.

Mistakes have been made, doubtless, in giving, and much money has, through insufficient thought, been given unwisely. Much which has been given in such manner, as to do some good, might, with greater wisdom, have been so given as to have accomplished greater good. Still, it is true that we have heard altogether too much about the difficulties of giving, and thus there has been a tendency to dry up the springs of generosity. It is stated here and there that it is becoming more and more difficult to raise money for good works, and the number of givers remains comparatively small on the contribution lists for benevolent enterprises; in all our cities, the same names recur again and again.

The greatest difficulty in giving is in giving to individuals who are needy. Anything of the kind, especially in the form of almsgiving, is difficult, and it is doubtless true that it would be difficult for a millionaire himself to give away in alms anything like one hundred thousand dollars a year, and to give it helpfully. This giving to needy individuals requires personal contact and personal knowledge. It is to overcome the difficulties of giving of this kind that Charity Organization Societies have been established, and that we have developed what is called scientific charity.

Perhaps it may be laid down, as a general rule, that giving to individuals is especially the function of those who themselves are poor, or only moderately well-to-do. A very rich man, almost of necessity, gets too far away from needy individuals to help them. As his wealth increases he grows away from the needy, and, moreover, he is especially liable to imposition.

Yet, there are many different ways of giving, and it is not easy to feel that any earnest man can find it difficult to give advantageously all the surplus which he is able to spare, even if he adheres most rigidly to Christian principles in regard to his own expenditures and those of his family. If one is a believer in foreign and domestic missions—and no one can fail to believe in both who accepts Christianity—a way at once is opened to him for the expenditure of millions of money. It is said that even now nearly, if not quite all, of our boards of missions are in debt.

When we turn to educational enterprises the opportunities for giving are simply unlimited. A man may well take time in order to choose between various objects presented, but there is no lack of opportunity for disposal of more millions than any living human being has. The writer sees how, in the institution with which he is connected, millions could be expended wisely. And probably there is no professor in any institution in our land who would not undertake to use all the money that could be placed at his disposal. What are the things that occur to the writer? One or two may be mentioned : Scholarships and fellowships, as an aid to gifted young men and women in the development of their faculties for social service; a building for the Young Men's and Young Women's Christian Associations, as a headquarters for their religious work among the fifteen hundred students in his own university; dormitories, established and maintained by Christian people, under Christian influences, which would be genuine homes for the young men and young women in this institution; an adequately endowed department of Economics and Politics which would be as amply equipped for its work as any department of Natural Science. These are illustrations which might be continued indefinitely.

When we turn to free public libraries, and think of the good that has been accomplished by their establishment in different communities, and of the large number of communities in the

Our Spendings. 243

country without such an educational institution, we see here, likewise, almost unlimited opportunities for giving. One hundred million dollars could be wisely expended within a year in establishing free public libraries in different cities of the United States. The entire South is almost destitute of the blessings of free public libraries.

But mention of the South reminds us again of its large Negro population, and also its large, illiterate white population, both of which need aid in the development of educational and religious institutions.

The common schools of the country are in many particulars inferior, and millions of money could be wisely used in their development and improvement. A far larger proportion of individual effort and private philanthropy ought to be turned in this direction. A few years ago some philanthropists in Boston contributed money to add new features, like cooking, to the public schools. They defrayed the expenses of the experiment, and when the stage of experimentation was passed the work was taken up and carried forward by the taxpayers. Private philanthropy has likewise encouraged the establishment of kindergartens, bearing the entire expense until the taxpayer could be educated up to an adequate appreciation of their mission. This is philanthropy of the most fruitful sort.

We have also our denominational schools and colleges which, like the public schools, must be reckoned with as a permanent force. Their funds are inadequate, and even with a wise policy of consolidation and co-operation with public institutions, like that pursued in some quarters, their needs are pressing and large, and afford a field for wise giving. Especially must one remember that theological training is exclusively committed to private efforts, and the endowments of our theological schools are sadly inadequate. At a time like the present, when the demands on the pulpit are becoming so vast, training schools for pastors and preachers must especially appeal to the thoughtful Christian of means.

If we turn to the slums of our cities, we find there countless thousands who need our help, and who can be saved from their evil surroundings by efforts of the right sort. It has been proved, by experience of the Children's Aid Societies and other agencies, that the majority of the children living in the slums can be brought up to lead useful and honorable lives if their surroundings are changed and right influences brought to bear upon them. "Save the children to-day, and you have saved the nation to-morrow." In the redemption of the slums of our cities we have opportunities for the application of social service of many times the number of workers now found in them, and also for the use of millions upon millions of money.

The work, however, which is to be done, cannot be done by any one class in the community alone; each one is responsible according to his talents, whatever they may be. It will not do for the rest of the community to stand aside and wait for millionaires to take action. A poor person with very small material resources can often accomplish a large work. Moreover, it is always unwise for the wealthy by their gifts to take responsibility off the shoulders of others. Several rich men recently, in giving to institutions, have made it a condition that others should make contributions also. One of the wealthy men of the United States, whose favorite form of benevolence is public libraries, says that he does not think it worth while to give a public library to any city which is not willing to tax itself for the support of the institution. The readiness of most of us to appeal to the wealthy, and to roll upon them all the public burdens which they are willing to carry, suggests a disposition which is a counterpart of the niggardliness of some rich men. It is always well to bear in mind what has been so frequently and so wisely said concerning the importance of helping others to help themselves.

It would be possible to continue the discussion

of the opportunities for giving, both material means and personal services, indefinitely. There are about us those who need our help of both kinds, as well as institutions which can be advantageously sustained and strengthened. All our resources are insufficient for the work which lies ready at our hand. Now, as ever, "the harvest truly is plenteous, but the laborers are few,"[1] and their resources are inadequate.

[1] Matthew ix, 37.

CHAPTER XIII.
WHAT TO DO.

"And respecting human feelings generally, I think that we may lay down this law : That in proportion as they are exerted on higher objects, they may safely be allowed to grow more and more intense; there can be no danger in our loving God too much, if only we understand His true nature, nor any possibility of abuse in devoting our lives for the good of man, if only we know the means by which that good is to be attained."—*Jowett, College Sermons, p.* 162.

"Men formerly thought that the simple direct action of the benevolent instincts by means of self-denying gifts was enough to remedy the misery they deplored ; now we see that not only thought, but historical study is also necessary."—*Arnold Toynbee, The Industrial Revolution in England, p.* 94.

"When you have found your work, whatever it be, give yourself to it with all your heart, and make the resolution in God's sight never to go to your rest leaving a stone unturned which may help your aims. Half-and-half charity does very little good to the objects; and is a miserable, slovenly affair for the workers. And when the end comes and the night closes in, the long, last night of earth, when no man can work any more in this world, your milk-and-water, half-hearted charities will bring no memories of comfort to you. They are not so many 'good works' which you can place on the credit side of your account, in the mean, commercial spirit taught by some of the Churches. Nay, rather, they are only solemn evidences that you *knew your duty*, knew you *might* do good, and did it not, or did it half-heartedly! What a thought for those last days when we know ourselves to be going home to God, God—whom at bottom, after all, we have loved and shall love forever—that we *might* have served Him here, *might* have blessed His creatures, *might* have done His will on earth as it is done in heaven, but we have let the glorious chance slip by us forever."—*Life of Frances Power Cobbe, by Herself, pp.* 554, 555.

CHAPTER XIII.

WHAT TO DO.

THE demand for a practical program is a natural one. One will say, "Here am I, a clerk in a drygoods house; what must I do?" Another, "Here am I, a worker on a farm; what does the social message of Christianity mean for me?" Another will say, "I am a teacher; what is the thing for me to do now, and here?" So representatives of various industrial classes, the pastor, the merchant, the legislator, the judge, all ask the question, "What have I to do if I would follow the social teachings of Christianity?" What are the practical conclusions drawn from the general principles which have been already elaborated?

A complete guide of conduct is out of the question. We have liberty, and with liberty goes responsibility. No one can keep at our elbow perpetually, turning us now in this direction, now in that; we would then become automata and not free personalities; we would, indeed, become things and not persons at all. No problem that presents itself is precisely like a previous problem, and we must decide the problems as they arise, seeking such aid as we can find within our reach. We have the inner light, and we have available a vast amount of positive knowledge based upon reflection and experience.

Nevertheless, helpful suggestions of a general character may be given; in regard to some things we may be clear. The way in which we must travel is not altogether without signposts affording needful directions.

We speak about social righteousness, but for each person the beginning is found in personal salvation. It is safe to give this advice: Bring yourself into right relations with God; that is the beginning of all things. Through this right relationship with God, seek to enter into right relations with your fellows. If we begin otherwise, it is impossible to tell where we will end. Humanitarianism by itself—that is to say, humanitarianism which does not rest back upon God—is as unstable as the sands. The enthusiasm of humanity of to-day may end to-morrow in cold egoism. The question naturally soon suggests itself, "Why, after all, should I trouble myself about my neighbors; my efforts seem to accomplish little, and, after all, man is a poor creature." It is only in Christ that man is exalted. Apart from Christ the natural tendency is to come back to the standpoint of the Greeks and despise the masses.

What to Do. 251

We need to keep close to Christ to avoid the dangers which beset each one of us. Whatever our situation, it has its peculiar dangers. We have seen how much is expected of us, and we are reminded that Christ said, "Narrow is the way." We have found how great the responsibility of a rich man, and how difficult for him to conform to the law of mutual love in his earnings and in his expenditures, and we are reminded that Christ said that it was easier for a camel to go through the needle's eye than for a rich man to enter into the kingdom. But the poor also have their peculiar dangers, and especially so at the present time when so much social agitation of an evil character is going forward. Envy is a social force pulling men down, and this is observable at every turn at the present time; it is one of the things making our public life poor and mean. It shows itself in a communism of the worst type which, instead of pulling men up, wants to pull all down to a common level, and reduce every manifestation of excellence to a wretched mediocrity.

Each one may well bear in mind the parable of the fig tree: If it bears fruit, it is good; if not, it is hewn down. If we receive Christ in our heart, and then do not go to work to bear fruit; if we do not help and comfort others; if we fail to minister to those about us, to show mercy unto prisoners and captives, then the sap of life dries up, the life in us dies, we wither away and lose that which we had. It is a condition of life that we must pass on what we receive, and pass it on enlarged. "Blessed be God, . . . who comforteth us in all our tribulations, that we may be able to comfort them which are in any trouble."[1]

In our practical activity, there are no words more useful to keep in mind than these: "The next thing." Do the next thing. Generally this is something definite and concrete; possibly not something large and grand, yet who can tell? The story of the leper general is typical. He was told to wash in the waters of a little brook. This was something so simple that it was rejected in scorn. Some great and difficult thing was wanted. The work of everyone tells. Society is an organism made up of interdependent parts, each one in itself a living organism. We have to work both ways: downward to the parts, and upward to the whole. At any moment what can be done will find fixed limits in the character of the individuals who comprise the whole. Every improvement in your own character and in your own surroundings is an improvement for every circle, large and small, of which you form a part. Every helpful word, every kind deed, is a contribution to the perfection of society. We must be care-

[1] 2 Corinthians i, 3, 4.

What to Do. 253

ful, lest we despise small things. We may read of the grand work of a man like Charles Loring Brace, the soul of the Children's Aid Society of New York city, and feel discouraged, or think our own sphere of action too small, when we are told that he rescued hundreds of thousands of children. A spirit of despondency, possibly, may seize us if we read an account of the vastly larger work of the seventh Earl of Shaftesbury, and learn that the factory legislation which he did so much to bring about, and his other social efforts, changed greatly the life of England, benefiting millions of human beings in his own lifetime, and many more millions unborn at the time of his death. Their deeds were grand, indeed, and all honor to them! But what social conditions made their beneficent activity possible? When we reflect carefully upon this question, we discover that millions toiled to make their deeds a possibility. The next thing is the thing for each one. If we take a step at a time, always doing the next thing, and walk forward in the right path, we may find that finally we have traveled a long distance; and one thing is certain, and that is, in the end we will receive the plaudit, "Well done."

The work for a student is to do his best as a student, acquiring what he can. The thing for the carpenter to do is to become the best possible carpenter, feeling that his calling is a calling of

God; that he is, indeed, a carpenter by the grace of God. If a way opens for something which seems larger and brings greater emoluments, very well; but good carpenters, good blacksmiths, good farmers, as well as good lawyers, judges, and congressmen, have an honorable work, and if their tasks are well discharged their work will help bring in the kingdom.

Another word—"Seek light." Misguided enthusiasm may do more harm than good. We are responsible for the use of our intellectual as well as our emotional natures. It is for us to use such opportunities as we have to know what should be done, and how it should be done. We must remember how Christ reproached the professedly religious people of His day with blindness, and how grievous a sin in His eyes was this blindness. "Ye blind guides," "Ye fools and blind," "Ye fools and blind," "Ye blind guides," "Thou blind Pharisee"—these all occur in a single discourse—an awful sermon of condemnation, the like of which in its severe denunciation has, perhaps, never been surpassed. "Get wisdom, and with all thy getting, get understanding."[1] We are told that wisdom is the principal thing; and if we interpret wisdom largely enough, this is true. "Look and see," is the injunction of an economist who believed in observation. It

[1] Proverbs iv, 7.

is a good motto. "Look and see." We must read the Bible, and we must read the lives of those who have done great things; the lives of servants of God, like Elizabeth Fry, John Howard, and the seventh Earl of Shaftesbury.[1] Methods of conspicuously successful soldiers of the cross are to be studied. Our Church is a Church militant, and tactics may not be neglected. Our meetings together should be meetings in which to lay plans for work, and meetings in which reports should be made of work done. Reports should be made of poor succored and children rescued from evil surroundings, and of almshouses, jails, and prisons visited.

We may take up our various social circles, one after the other, and seek to apply our general principles in each one of them. For the individual, the first social circle is the family. This is the social cell, and must be regarded from the social point of view. Multiplied divorces are a natural outcome of an individualistic point of view of the family. It may seem hard that two incompatible natures should be obliged to live together and should not separate, and each one

[1] Especially the latter, as he is a man of our own times, and his work is peculiarly instructive for us. See *Life and Work of the Seventh Earl of Shaftesbury*, by Edwin Hodder, in three volumes. Cassell & Company, New York, 1886. The work is exceedingly entertaining, and should not fail to be in every Sunday school library.

join itself to a congenial and helpful nature; but the social point of view at once forces home the question, What are the social consequences? To this question there can be only one answer, and that completely vindicates the law of Christ with respect to divorce. We are to build up in every way the family, providing for our own, and not drawing the line too closely about those whom we consider members of our own family. There is a tendency at present to a decay of family feeling, and even close relationship is too frequently forgotten when there is an occasion for helpful service, although vividly enough remembered when an estate is to be divided among heirs! We have, in considerations based upon the family, a guide for a large proportion of our social conduct. A sound family life implies a right physical environment, and this brings before us sanitary reform in all our cities. Improved drainage, small parks, playgrounds, may be mentioned. Saloons and brothels in the neighborhood of the home and the school mean a poisoned environment. It is particularly the poor who suffer in this respect, as was well brought forward before the American Federation of Labor at its recent convention by a representative of the Women's Christian Temperance Union. It appears that in New York, some time ago, there was one liquor saloon to 200 inhabitants, but in the slum district one saloon to 129 persons; in Philadelphia the figures were 870 and 502; in Baltimore, 229 and 105; in Chicago, 212 and 127.[1]

Conditions of work may also be examined from the standpoint of the family. If the father toils fifteen, sixteen, and seventeen hours a day, as happened a few years ago in the case of the street-car employees of Baltimore, it must be at the expense of the family. It is impossible that he should discharge his duties to his family when he scarcely sees his own children awake for weeks at a time. If wage-earners toil seven days in a week, this can only be at the expense of the family. If work on other days is so hard that Sunday is used simply for recovery from physical exhaustion, then the family is deprived of religious influences. If little children who should be in school are at work in shops and factories, and the mothers are obliged to leave home for the support of the family, then this, likewise, can only tend to the decay of the family. When we discuss the children in the family which should be a shield to them, a bulwark of defense against evils, a garden in which they may grow up into manhood and womanhood surrounded by all

---

[1] See the article on "Our Slums," by Dr. J. H. W. Stuckenberg, *Homiletic Review*, October, 1895; also, "Labor and Temperance," by Mrs. J. H. W. Stuckenberg, in the *American Federationist*, of Indianapolis, January, 1896.

good influences, we think of the bad environment which poisons childhood so frequently, and we remember Christ's solicitude for little children: "Whoso shall offend one of these little ones which believe in Me, it were better for him that a millstone were hanged about his neck, and that he were drowned in the depth of the sea."[1] If we have eyes to see, we cannot fail to discern conditions all about us, those mentioned and many others, which cause our little ones to stumble, and every one is responsible precisely in so far as he has not given heed to these conditions, and done what in him lies to remedy them. We have here brought before us vast evils, and some way out of them must be discovered. There is wisdom enough in the churches for the solution of these problems, if it is earnestly applied to them.

The mention of the Church brings before us another social circle which must be yeast in society, leavening the whole. The work of the Church becomes immensely more difficult with the complexity of modern society. Pastors and preachers have a natural leadership in the work of the Church, and the vastness of this work suggests the need of strong men in the pulpit. But the laity, also, have their work. It is not for them simply to receive, but for

[1] Matthew xviii, 6.

them also to feel like responsibility with their leaders. It is for all in the Church to make her a fit bride of Christ.

The Church must hold before herself her ideal as a transforming power for righteousness. Righteousness means rightness—right relations toward God and man. It is, perhaps, significant that we have come to use the word "religion" more frequently than "righteousness." They may mean the same things; but it is suggestive that in the Bible the word "religion" is used three times, and the word "righteousness" more than one hundred times three times. Probably the modern Christian uses the word "religion" at least ten times as often as the word "righteousness." The ultimate ideal, so far as we can gather from the prophets and the Book of Revelation, is the Church as the all-embracing form of association for every kind of social work. But this must mean a oneness of Church and State, as we have already mentioned. This implies a complete transformation and change from anything that we now know, and we have to build up each one of these great divine institutions in its own sphere. We have work in the Church to do which we may call extensive, bringing others into relations with the Church and increasing its members.

But quite as important is intensive work, to

be conducted, not ostentatiously, but quietly. This is the field for individual and social effort. This is the kind of work which the Epworth League, the Christian Endeavor Societies, St. Andrew's Brotherhood, and other organizations are all doing, and will do, we may hope, more effectively in the future. Through these organizations individual power may be brought to bear upon the life of the Church. We criticise the Church, not as an ideal organization, but as an actual organization of those who profess Christianity; and we do so rightly. Yet there is no reason why we should despair of the Church, but quite the contrary. We may also say, so far as the relations of anyone to his individual Church is concerned, that a change should not lightly be made. The work to do is extensive and intensive.

It is a great thing to work through the Church. We have in the Church an immense organization, built up by the efforts of generation upon generation for well-nigh nineteen hundred years. We have an organization which will endure, and efforts put into this organization will last.

Within the Church it is for us to do good to those about us and to form a true brotherhood, so that men may say again, "How these Christians love one another!" At times a particular

What to Do. 261

church organization tends to become a fashionable club. Nothing could be further from the mind of Christ. The church is to exercise the widest hospitality. We are to attend the services of the church, not merely in plain but inexpensive attire, lest worldly discrimination should creep into the church, and our conduct become a stumbling-block to others.

But our work in the Church is the redemption of the world, not plucking a few out of the world. The Church must ever be remembered as leaven, leavening the entire lump. This suggests a true unity of Christians, working together on the world. If all institutions are to be redeemed, then it is important to remember that we have something far larger before us than merely the upbuilding of denominational institutions, important as these may be. It is for us to put the spirit of Christ into all social institutions. It is for Christians not only to exercise a care over the home for the aged which bears a denominational name, but over the county poorhouse. It is for Christians not only to exercise solicitude with respect to the church hospital, but to extend their watchfulness to the city hospital. It is for them not merely to build up the school of a religious sect, but the public school; not merely to care for the church college, but to see to it that the State university is all that it should be. We have a family selfishness, against which Christ warned us in His precepts and practice. But we have also a church selfishness which is equally contrary to the mind of Christ. Christ scarcely uttered the word "church," but the word "kingdom" was perpetually in His mouth. We must see to it that for us the church means the kingdom.

Coming back to our maxim, "The next thing," we may ask ourselves, "What is the 'next thing' in social work for the Church?" There is certainly no work of this nature less open to question and more pressing than that which is brought before us by charities and correction. Beneficence has in all ages been considered a peculiar feature of the life of the Church. It is especially mentioned that it is one object of the Epworth League to train young members and friends of the Church "in works of mercy and help."[1] No Christian organization has ever denied the duty of Christians with respect to charities and correction. This is work which can be only in a limited sense denominational

[1] It is interesting to read that John Wesley, Charles Wesley, George Whitefield, and other members of Oxford University formed a society and "began practical work with the prisoners in Oxford castle, visiting and comforting them in their confinement, helping the unfortunate debtors locked up in Bocardo, and paying for the education of poor children." Vide *English Social Reformers*, by H. de B. Gibbins, M.A., p. 78.

What to Do. 263

work. It is a work in which Christians must unite with one another, and enter into relations with public authorities and public institutions, if their work is to be fruitful. Yet, notwithstanding the clearest instructions from the founder of the Church and His apostles, notwithstanding all our professions, there is the strangest neglect of those most wretched and unhappy classes of human beings for whom charities and correction exist. We pray continually for "fatherless children and widows, and all who are desolate and oppressed." A great deal of charitable work is accomplished; but much of it is so unintelligent, that the question is often raised whether it does more harm than good. What we are instructed to do is to consider the poor and needy, endeavoring always so to help men as to prevent the evil of pauperism, and to cure it where it does exist.[1] That is what we do not do, for we put

[1] In anticipation of a plea often urged for an evasion of social duties it may be observed in this connection : First, that Christ did not say, "The poor ye *shall* always have with you." He used the present tense, pointing to a present fact. The poor were always present with them. Second, poverty is one thing, pauperism is another. Thoughtful people are beginning to feel that there is no reason why pauperism should continue, although relatively poor people will always be with us, and there can never be a time when mutual helpfulness will not be needed. We have abundant experience to show us that pauperism can be exterminated, if an earnest and intelligent and general effort is made to accomplish this purpose. Third, if the poor are always with us, this is

little heart and less mind into our charitable and correctional work. If it is proposed to consider the charitable and correctional work of a city full of churches, and the wisest and most experienced men in these lines of work come to impart to those who are gathered together lessons derived from their wisdom and experience, it is extremely difficult to gather together an audience for those things which ought to concern Christians most deeply. It would be something to create surprise if, in a city with fifty churches, one of them could be filled on such an occasion. The management of public charitable and correctional institutions is of the most vital concern to the most needy, and in some cases the most helpless, members of the community. In some instances, as in the case of the feeble-minded and the insane, we have, indeed, to do with those who are utterly helpless. Trained workers of high character may do a great deal for those thousands of unhappy beings in every commonwealth in the Union. Management of the reverse kind works immeasurable harm and unspeakable cruelty. Nevertheless, so neglectful have the churches

no excuse for our neglect of the problem of poverty. Quite the contrary is taught in the Bible. The statement in Deuteronomy, that "the poor shall never cease out of the land," is immediately followed by this injunction: "Therefore, I command thee, saying, Thou shalt open thine hand wide unto thy brother, to thy poor, and to thy needy in thy land" (Exodus xv, 11).

What to Do. 265

been of charities and correction, that they raise no general, forceful protest when offices connected with these institutions are made the spoils of partisan politics and distributed, not on the basis of merit, but as "plums," or "pie," or "fat;" expressions used every day in the press, but indicating a low moral level of public life.[1] It will

[1] Not long since three men held important offices in Illinois, which were concerned with the administration of charitable and correctional institutions. These men had held these offices for many years, and had become recognized throughout the entire country as distinguished authorities in their field. They were an honor to their State, and their activity was beneficent to those unfortunate classes placed under their charge. When partisan politics removed these men, there was no protest on the part of the churches of which the author has been able to discover any trace. When recently partisan politics, instead of tried and approved fitness, decided appointments in an industrial school, insane asylums, and the school for the blind in Wisconsin, the Christian people of the State, except in the case of a few individuals, had nothing to say. Shall we blame the politicians? A politician who may regret the existing condition of affairs can well say: "I am powerless. There is no evidence of any sentiment in the State which would support me, should I do what is really desirable in the matter of these appointments." The answer may not be entirely satisfactory, but the blame rests chiefly on the churches, for if they were deeply interested and watchful, these things would be impossible. When societies like the Epworth League, the Christian Endeavor Societies, and St. Andrew's Brotherhood become aroused on subjects of this kind, these things will have to cease. Politicians of the better sort will rejoice, and politicians of the baser sort will be powerless to prevent righteousness in their appointments to these public offices.

not do to say that we have not thought of these things, for we are put here, and given minds and hearts that we may think of them. The condemnation is, "Inasmuch as ye did it not unto one of the least of these."

It may be well to give some definite and precise methods to be followed by those who would arouse an intelligent interest on the part of Christian people in charities and correction, and who would stimulate right action. The following suggestions are offered: First, study the results of experience and thought, as presented in two excellent books on these subjects, namely: Warner's *American Charities* and Wines's *Punishment and Reformation*. A class may be formed taking up first Dr. Warner's book, chapter by chapter, and then Dr. Wines's work. All persons who can be found willing to "lend a hand" should be asked to join the class. From time to time some one with special knowledge or experience may be invited to address the class on that topic with which he or she has become familiar. Jails, poorhouses, insane asylums, police stations in cities, are topics which occur at once to the mind. Then when some knowledge has been gained, all institutions of this character which can be reached should be visited, their actual administration studied, and their needs discovered. Work will be found in abundance. On the one hand there will be inmates of institutions to be visited regularly, and it may come about that on visiting lists of ladies will be found those who now are hungry for what can be given in cheerful and helpful words. Hospitality, which is praised by the Apostle Paul, may be extended in directions indicated in the New Testament. On the other hand, evils and abuses will be discovered, and after these are thoroughly understood they may be brought before the public and kept before the public until remedied. And if wherever there is a Christian church, or even wherever there is a branch of the Epworth League, or a Christian Endeavor Society, there are at least one or two who understand these questions and are alive to their import, whenever it is proposed to use public offices in charitable and correctional institutions as "pie" and "fat," there will arise such a mighty cry, "Hands off," that no politician will dare to disobey it.

If we open the Prayer Book of the Protestant Episcopal Church, or Wesley's *Sunday Service*, we find this petition: "That it may please thee to preserve all who travel by land or water, all women in the perils of childbirth, all sick persons, and young children; and to show thy pity upon all prisoners and captives; We beseech thee to hear us, good Lord." It may be supposed that like prayers may be heard in every church. How much social reform is embraced in this one petition? How much social work does it suggest, if, indeed, we are to work for that for which we pray? "All who travel by land or water"—railway employees, exposed to needless jeopardy every hour; likewise railway passengers; also stokers and other employees of steamship companies, whose environment is notoriously bad. The preservation of all who travel by land or sea involves a goodly proportion of needed reform. "All women in the perils of childbirth," and "young children," remind us, among other things, of needed sanitary reforms, for unsanitary conditions imperil both classes, destroying, needlessly, the lives of hundreds of thousands yearly. "Young children" suggests the abuses of factory labor on the one hand, and the improvement of schools on the other; also the opportunities for helpful, life-giving enjoyment.

The labor movement and the Church is a fruitful topic. Everywhere the question is asked, "What attitude shall the Church take with respect to the labor movement?" The Church, as such, can, to be sure, take comparatively few positions, and these must relate, for the most part, rather to ends to be accomplished than to methods to be followed in the accomplishment of these ends. But certain general things can be made

What to Do.

clear. The aims of life for wage-earners and all others should be held before us. The social doctrines of the entire Bible may be explained, bringing into right relations the Old and the New Testament. The Bible doctrine of land is one of importance. It is well said of "the law given from God by Moses" that the civil precepts thereof ought not "of necessity be received in any commonwealth." This would imply an adoption of institutions which are not adapted to modern conditions, and which would accomplish results quite contrary to the purposes of these civil precepts. But the permanent spirit of them must again and again be brought before us, remembering that Christianity always means more kindness than Judaism, not less; more generosity, not less; more love to all men, not less to any man.

It is not easy for the writer to understand how a preacher, as a preacher, can advocate at the present time anything in regard to which there are such differences of opinion on the part of good men, and in regard to which there is so much uncertainty, as the single tax. The same may be said with respect to socialism, in a narrow sense, implying specific schemes for reform. On the other hand, for the sake of social peace, such schemes may occasionally be described with impartiality and their religious aspects explained.

Certain ideals which both the single tax and socialism place before men are implied unquestionably in Christianity. Each man is to be treated, not as a means to an end, but as an end in himself; each man is to be given the best opportunities for the development of all faculties, and the utmost sympathy must be shown for all efforts to elevate truly the masses of men. It can also well be pointed out how vast are the new responsibilities brought upon us by our increasing wealth. Certain ideals which would have once been out of the question are now brought within the realm of practical discussion by our larger productive power. A question like the eight-hour day will serve as an example. The Church, as Church, can scarcely take a position at the present time in regard to anything so definite and precise, and so uncertain in its results. It can, however, well be brought forward that a question of this kind means something different now from what it could have meant in earlier days. It is a question of how we can best utilize the new opportunities given by greater power in the production of wealth. It can also be clearly shown that if the larger productive power of labor is consumed simply in greater luxury and self-indulgence, then the decay of nations which past ages have witnessed will inevitably continue, and a grave will close over the national powers of to-day, as it has over the many nations which were once the admiration of the world, but have now utterly perished. Peace is also something which can be promoted by the Church, as Church, and this will be effected if the aims and aspirations of the labor movement are understood, and if the perplexities and difficulties of various classes are brought forward. It is not for the preacher to a congregation of wage-earners to dwell merely upon the shortcomings of employers and the vices of the wealthy; nor is it for the preacher to wealthy congregations so much to hold up the alleged wickedness of walking delegates, as to help his congregation to know what the workingmen really want, and to enforce upon the wealthy their own vast responsibilities.

We may, in short, "study in common how to apply the moral truths and principles of Christianity to the social and economic difficulties of the present time," and we may " present Christ in practical life as the Living Master and King, the enemy of wrong and selfishness, the power of righteousness and love."

It has been suggested that certain Sundays may be set apart for the consideration of social topics from the Christian point of view. Many cities already have a hospital Sunday, and everywhere at least one sermon a year may be devoted to charities and correction. It has been recommended that the Sunday before the first Monday in September (the Sunday before Labor Day) should be devoted to the labor problem, and this recommendation has been followed with good results in at least a few churches. The first Sunday in May may also appropriately be used for some such purpose, inasmuch as generally throughout the world wage-earners are inclined to look upon the 1st of May as an international labor day. If still a fourth Sunday should be set apart for the consideration of a civic topic it would be little enough when we remember the importance Christ attached to whatever concerned the well-being of the masses of men, for we must not forget that all his miracles were wrought to relieve pain and sorrow and to promote physical and mental happiness. There was a higher purpose, but the occasions of the miracles surely are not without significance.

If we encourage those who have the opportunities and the brains to carry on studies designed to show what the Gospel means in all the details of modern life, if we take pains to keep in touch with them, if we take up in our churches the next things, those about which least difference of opinion exists on the part of conscientious and well-informed persons, as, for example, charities and correction, and child-saving in our cities, also the question of the homes of the people and the efforts to improve the dwellings of the poor, treating the moral bearings of this problem, helping the formation of social settlements, where the fortunate may learn the needs of those less fortunate, and minister to them; if we then pass on to the problem of the wage-earner, dealing first with the demands least open to question, as the demand for a rest day once a week, the demand for leisure for duties in the family every day and for the satisfaction of the higher needs of our nature, then to the various phases of the temperance problem, then to righteousness in civic affairs, feeling our way cautiously, but advancing at the same time fearlessly, we shall find our vision continually growing larger, and our field of work broadening out and finally including the entire life of human society.

When we come to individual Christians, then we also enter the sphere of methods as well as aims. If a Christian believes that the single tax will accomplish what is claimed for it, then he is bound to advocate it at the proper time and in the proper place. The same holds with regard to many other questions of the day, even with respect to the temperance question. We may safely go as far as the Discipline of the Methodist Episcopal Church goes, and say that it is for the family, the Church, and the State to work together for the success of the temperance reform. We must be very clear in our own minds about methods before we can insist upon precise political methods to be promoted by the Church.

A high citizenship suggests another line of work. Here, again, what the Church can do finds its limitations, and yet within these limits the field for the Church is a vast one. The old New England custom of election sermons preached before each election is entirely in keeping with the teachings of Christianity. At such a time it can be pointed out what moral issues are involved, what the State means, and whence the State derives its authority. The ideals of the State can be held up to men; a love of country can be inculcated as a part of Christianity, and a very important part. And this love, real and genuine, showing itself, not so much in loud talk as in deeds, is a condition precedent to any permanent and decided improvement in citizenship.

For it is true that those who place civic reform simply upon a business basis have not yet taken one step in the road which will lead to the attainment of their goal. Aristotle, even before the time of Christianity, was wise enough to recognize that the affairs of the nation were something far larger than business affairs in any narrow sense, and that the aim of citizenship was something higher than the acquisition of wealth. It is true that private aims and the commercial spirit, when dominant, lead to political degradation and not to purification. It is said, for example, "the government of the city is business, not politics." No one can point to any great and enduring triumph achieved on this basis. It will not fire the heart of the masses upon whom, in the long run, the life of the nation, in all its various spheres, must rest. What does business mean to the wage-earner? He hears the expression, "Business is business," and down go his wages ten per cent. "Business is business," and the factory is closed. "Business is business," and he is offered permanent employment in the service of the city on condition that he will support a corrupt faction. The author well remembers meeting a barber in Berlin, who had once been a citizen of the United States. The conversation turned upon the approaching elections in Germany, and the writer asked the barber whether he was going to vote. "Why should I vote?" was the reply. "I do not concern myself with politics, nobody gives me anything for my vote. When I was in New York I always got five dollars for my vote, and that was a different thing." This is a natural outcome of the downward tendency of the maxim, "Business is business," when introduced into politics. Let us take, however, the larger idea of the city as a household, and we have something upon which we can build. This idea means larger life, and it awakens genuine patriotism; that is to say, real love for one's country. A deservedly popular writer[1] has well said, "Without reverence and love citizenship cannot exist." We must have a feeling for our city, for our country, like that which is inculcated in the Bible. Our Jerusalem must be so dear to us that we can say with the psalmist, "If I forget thee, O Jerusalem, let my right hand forget her cunning.

"If I do not remember thee, let my tongue cleave to the roof of my mouth; if I prefer not Jerusalem above my chief joy."[2]

When we reach this point, then we shall attain civic reform; then our commonwealths will be regenerated; then shall we see our nation a new nation, exalted by righteousness.

[1] Ian Maclaren.   [2] Psalm cxxxvii, 5, 6.

www.ingramcontent.com/pod-product-compliance
Lightning Source LLC
Chambersburg PA
CBHW031947230426
43672CB00010B/2083